Light on

The Story of Gatehead Methodist Church

Julia Hinchliffe

2012

© Julia Hinchliffe 2012

ISBN 978 1 904446 42 2

British Library Cataloguing in Publication Data
Julia Hinchliffe 2012
Light on a Hill

Printed and published by
Quacks Books
7 Grape Lane, Petergate
York YO1 7HU

Come, let us to the hills! Where none but God
Can overlook us; for I hate to breathe
The breaths and think the thoughts of other men,
In close and clouded cities, where the sky
Frowns like an angry Father mournfully.
I love the hills and I love loneliness,
And Oh! I love the woods, those natural fanes
Whose very air is holy; and we breathe
Of God; for He doth come in special place,
And, while we worship, He is there for us!

FESTUS: A Poem, *by Philip James Bailey*

This book is dedicated to
the members of
Gatehead Methodist Church

Pat and Michael England
Ada Goddard
Donald Haigh
Amos Kaye
Winnie and John Robinson
Frank and Joyce Rollin
Margaret Sanderson
Margaret Smith
Barbara and Jeffrey Turner
Doris Mary Wagstaff
Barbara Wood

and to the memory of

Janey Armitage
Annie Kaye

Semper fidelis

Introduction and Acknowledgements

For nearly two centuries, a Methodist congregation has met faithfully week by week in a little chapel on the wind-swept hillside above Holmfirth in West Yorkshire. A few families, farmers, miners and weavers, built a chapel there in the early days of Primitive Methodism and the story of their lives is intimately connected to that of their church.

Gatehead was for years the focus of the life of its community, growing to accommodate their increasing numbers and watching over their lives from the baptismal font to the graveyard. It sent out preachers into the locality and ministers the length of the country and beyond. Generations of children followed their parents and grandparents into membership. But today, the national decline in church attendance has finally caught up with it and despite the valiant efforts of its remaining members to maintain the witness at Gatehead, its future is in increasing jeopardy.

Whatever the future may bring, this book is written so that the story of Gatehead and its people over the past two hundred years is not lost and the contribution they made to the area in which they lived is not forgotten.

My thanks go first and foremost to a man I never met but without whom this book could not have been written. Harold Battye attended Gatehead Chapel from infancy and served over the years as its treasurer and as a trustee. To mark each of three significant anniversaries of the chapel and the Sunday school, he compiled commemorative booklets recalling the history of the church and its people. This was no easy task as, in his own words, the earliest members of Gatehead Chapel 'kept the faith but not the records' and he had very little written material upon which to draw. Instead, he relied on his own memories of being brought

1

up at Gatehead, as well as the reminiscences of his mother and other older members of the church, and on his own research.

Harold Battye was also a talented artist and his drawings and paintings are used throughout this book. For this, I am very grateful to Harold's nephew, Leslie Tinker, who also allowed me to use family photographs and spent several hours talking me through them, sharing his memories of his uncle and other members of the chapel whom he knew well. Leslie also lent me his copies of Harold's booklets, which have formed the cornerstone upon which this book was built.

I am especially grateful to Jeffrey Turner, who entrusted me with his personal collection of photographs and memorabilia of Gatehead Chapel and who has always been available, despite the many calls on his time, to advise and encourage. Jeffrey also spent many hours proofreading the final manuscript and his comments and suggestions have made the resultant book both more comprehensive and more comprehensible.

My thanks also go to Michael and Pat England for proofreading the manuscript and for the corrections they made to it. Pat is now the longest serving member of the chapel, with Michael a close second, and they are the acknowledged authorities on its history. Both have given a lifetime's service to the care of the church and its members.

I am deeply grateful to my oldest friend, Mike Woods, for his support in this undertaking, as in all others. He kindly made space in his busy life to proofread the manuscript and his careful eye for detail led to the enhancement of both its content and structure. Dr Margaret Faull, Director of the National Coal Mining Museum for England, relinquished a rare opportunity for relaxation, during a train journey to Belgium, in order to cast an expert eye over the final copy. Her knowledge, as a published author, a historian and an authority on the mining industry, made her contribution invaluable and I owe her grateful thanks.

Leslie Robinson kindly allowed me to use some of the images he has accumulated over the course of a long lifetime and which now form part of the remarkable Textile Heritage Centre collection in Skelmanthorpe. I am most grateful to Richard Brook for showing me around the Centre and for his help in obtaining scans of the images.

Grateful thanks are also due to my friend and former pastor, Erroll Hulse, the author of many books, for his suggested reading. I deeply appreciate the encouragement of Colin Raynor and of local historian Pam Cooksey, who allowed me to use one of her illustrations. The patient assistance of the extremely helpful staff at Huddersfield Library's Local History Section and the Root Cellar in Meltham is also greatly appreciated.

I would like to thank my family for their support during the compilation of this history: my daughter, Becky, for her technical assistance and encouragement; my son, Rob, for washing his own shirts occasionally; and my husband, David, for being my eyes when I could not see.

Finally, I would like to thank all the members of Gatehead Methodist Church for the welcome they have given to me. Visitors to the church are always struck by their spontaneous adherence to the command of Jesus: 'As I have loved you, so you must love one another. By this, all men will know that you are my disciples'. (John 13:34-35, NIV).

All proceeds from the sale of this book will go to the chapel.

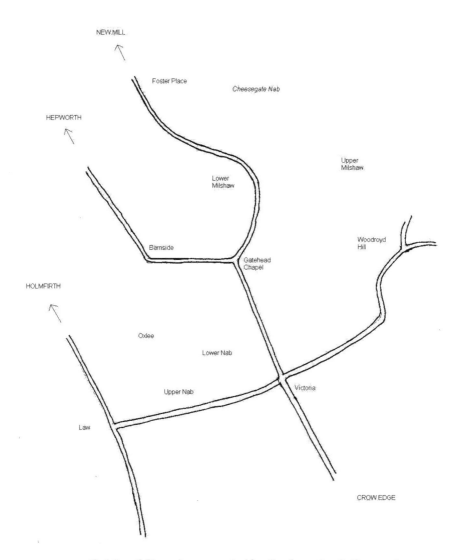

NEW MILL

Foster Place

Cheesegate Nab

HEPWORTH

Upper
Milshaw

Lower
Milshaw

Barnside

Woodroyd
Hill

Gatehead
Chapel

HOLMFIRTH

Oxlee

Lower Nab

Upper Nab

Victoria

Law

CROW EDGE

Gatehead Chapel surrounded by the farmsteads it served

The Setting

'A wilder people I never saw in England!'

This was John Wesley's reaction, recorded in his journal for 1757, as he rode through the hills above Huddersfield, where, some sixty years later, the first congregation of a little chapel called Gatehead would meet for the first time. 'The men, women and children filled the streets as we rode along,' he recalled, 'and appeared ready to devour us.'

John Wesley would have anticipated a warm welcome from his friend, Henry Venn, the vicar of Huddersfield Parish Church, but the folk he passed on his way had scant reason to cheer the arrival of a stranger. Little more than a decade after the last Jacobite rebellion and with Britain engaged in the Seven Years War over its trading and empirical interests in the colonies, visitors were viewed with suspicion and often dreaded for the news they might bring with them. The reaction of the Yorkshire villagers was not much different from that of ordinary people in many villages of that era, when the very fact of a traveller being unknown was seen as reason enough to set the dogs on him.[i]

In 1801 some 7268 people lived in Huddersfield, a conurbation described by one traveller as 'a miserable village, the houses poor and scattered, the streets narrow, crooked and dirty.'[ii] The little town had evolved in a piecemeal fashion rather than with structured planning and had an air of grime about it, 'the houses of the general people low-roofed, cramped, dark and almost indecent in the absence of conveniences'.[iii]

People were hungry. In June 1783 the price of corn was 60 shillings per quarter and the distress, particularly of the poorest members of society, led to corn riots in Bradford, Halifax and Huddersfield to demand an immediate reduction in the price of corn. Two of the leaders of the protest in Halifax, Thomas Spencer, 56, and Mark Saltonstall, aged just 19, were hanged on Beacon Hill, theirs the last public hangings in Halifax. In 1799 a soup kitchen was opened in Huddersfield to supply soup to the poor at a penny a quart, but even this was beyond the means of many and in November of that year 'gangs of desperate men seized what corn they could find in the warehouses and sold it at their own price'.[iv]

Little wonder then that ordinary folk should seek to enliven the drudgery of their existence at feast and fair time but even here the brutality of the age was reflected in the choice of entertainment. The favoured pastime of the day was bull fighting and there was a bullring at Lockwood built for the purpose. D F E Sykes, in his depiction of life in bygone Huddersfield, describes how many people kept bulldogs and mastiffs to match against the unfortunate bull, which was tied to a stake with ropes twenty feet long. The dog owners stood at the front of a baying crowd, pitting their animals in turn against the bull and cheering wildly when the agonised creature tossed one of them into the air. These dogs would also be matched against bears which were occasionally led into town for the purpose. The bears wore spiked collars around their necks to protect their throats, so that the dogs could not actually kill them and thus end their lives of misery and the profit of their owners. When a Bill prohibiting these practices was placed before Parliament in 1802, it was rejected, its opponents pleading that it would 'banish the pastime of the poor while leaving unchecked horse racing and hunting, the diversions of the rich'.[v] Cock-fighting, however, was widely practised by all classes of society. Like bull baiting, it was not finally banned until 1835 and even then was frequently still practised covertly.

Huddersfield was the centre of trade for the smaller towns and moorland villages which surrounded it. Cattle were bought and sold at the beast market, while nearby pieces of cloth were spread out for sale on the low walls of the parish church. Travelling to and from the town was itself fraught with danger. Clothiers taking their precious cloth to market faced many perils on the tortuous roads. Heavily laden horses and donkeys could stumble and injure themselves on the unmade trails and byways and carriages could break an axle and land in a ditch. But the danger which the journeying trader most dreaded was posed by the footpads and highwaymen who roamed the roads, ready to relieve him of his hard-earned money. Many a clothier, celebrating a profitable day's trading, found himself returning to his home and to his workers with nothing to show for it but a sore head, the effort of weeks, of men, women and children, wiped out in a momentary encounter.

Figure 1. Hand-loom weaving

Cloth production itself was evolving. For centuries it had remained more or less unchanged, generations of weavers following the same pattern of life as their ancestors had done. The whole family was involved. In their moorland cottages dotted on the hillside, separated by fields but within calling distance of each other, or in the villages in rows of weavers' cottages, women and children carded the wool and spun it into yarn. The men worked at the loom and stretched the resultant cloth onto tenter posts in the fields. Everyone helped in the process of dyeing the fabric in a large vat in the yard before it was taken on the back of a donkey to the fulling mill to be finished. Each family grew vegetables and corn and perhaps kept a pig, which was slaughtered in the autumn to provide meat through the winter. Perhaps they also kept a cow for milk and poultry for eggs. Life was hard but largely enjoyable. People felt a sense of satisfaction in providing for their own needs and in seeing the end product of their labours.

But with the introduction of mechanisation, life began to change. James Hargreaves patented the Spinning Jenny in 1770 and the first clothier in the Holme Valley to use one was James Beardsell of Holme in about 1776.[vi] The Spinning Jenny could spin dozens of times the amount of yarn that the old spinning wheels could manage, which in turn meant that more looms were required. Whereas previously ten spinners would have been needed to supply one weaver, now the Jenny produced all the yarn he could use. Third storeys with rows of small windows to provide sufficient light by which to work were added to the cottages to house the looms, producing the weavers' cottages that are characteristic of the Holme Valley today. On the heels of the Spinning Jenny came the carding and scribbling machine invented by Sir Richard Arkwright, which arrived in the Holme Valley in 1780. But these devices needed power to drive them. The answer, for the wealthier clothiers, was to build large mills in the valley bottoms (previously avoided because of the danger of flooding) where water power could turn the great wheels that powered the machines.

Figure 2. Looms were housed in the upper storeys of cottages where rows of windows provided maximum light

And so the centre of work for those engaged in cloth production gradually changed from the home to the factory, from the hills to the valleys, from the countryside to the towns. Young people who had grown to adulthood under the caring instruction of parents were now exposed to the atmosphere of the factory which was 'none too sweet and wholesome'.[vii] Their parents were put out of work as the machines took over. Everywhere, the introduction of mechanisation was greeted with fear, suspicion and, on occasion, violence. In 1812 groups of workers banded together under the supposed leadership of Ned Ludd and these so-called Luddites made night-time raids on the factories to smash the hated machines. As Britain was by now at war with France, the ports were closed, both to the importation of food and the exportation of goods and so hungry workers were laid off by manufacturers who could not sell their products. When the Napoleonic wars finally ended in 1815, hundreds of soldiers returned from fighting for their country to find themselves joining the ranks of the unemployed.

Their small hands, and the fact that they could be paid significantly less than adults, meant that many children were employed in the mills. Until the Factory Act was passed in 1833, making it illegal to employ children under the age of nine or for more than ten hours a day, boys and girls could work from six in the morning until ten at night, eating what meals they had as they did so. To keep them from falling asleep, an overlooker paced the rows with a strap. Parents frequently relied on the earnings of their children to keep the whole family out of the workhouse and so had little redress against the cruelties imposed on their offspring. Most piteous of all were the pauper children who had no parents to care for them and who could be sent from workhouses in towns miles away to be 'apprenticed' to a mill owner until the age of twenty-one. Such apprenticeships were little more than slavery, with any wages earned by the apprentice going to pay the supposed debt he owed to his master.

Giving evidence to the 1833 Royal Commission into the conditions of children working in factories,[viii] Abraham Whitehead, a clothier from Scholes, spoke of seeing local children setting off for work in the mills at five in the morning and returning after ten at night, so tired that they hardly knew what they were doing. He recalled that on one occasion, the child of a neighbour, Jonas Barrowcliffe, had been roused for work at two in the morning, having only arrived home at eleven. The family did not possess a clock and mistook the moonlight for dawn. Children were beaten or dismissed from their employment for arriving late and knowing the dire consequences for their families set out practically still asleep to walk for sometimes one or two hours to the mills. The hours worked left no time for education or even parental instruction and the moral welfare of the children consequently suffered. Abraham Whitehead recalled a boy of less than six living near him who, when he had earned a few coppers of his own, would take them to the ale house and order beer. As for the girls, a proverb became prevalent in Holmfirth: that any man wishing to marry should avoid choosing a 'factory doll' as, having spent all her time in the mills, she would not know how to manage a family.

Accidents were rife. Sleepy children were pulled into the machines and their little bodies crushed and ripped. Long hours standing at their task caused deformities in growing bones and the beatings received for any perceived transgression were frequently severe. And on the night of 14th February 1818, seventeen young girls between the ages of nine and eighteen years perished in the flames when Atkinson's Mill at Colne Bridge near Huddersfield caught fire. The children 'had been locked into the mill and it was generally stated and believed that when the flames broke out the key had been mislaid and could not be found.'[ix]

Elizabeth Barrett Browning gave voice to the plight of children labouring in mine and mill in her poem 'The Cry of the Children':

> *"For oh," say the children, "we are weary*
> *And we cannot run or leap -*
> *If we cared for any meadows, it were merely*
> *To drop down in them and sleep. . ."*
>
> *"How long," they say, "how long, O cruel nation*
> *Will you stand, to move the world, on a child's heart, -*
> *Stifle down with a mailed heel its palpitation*
> *And tread onward to your throne amid the mart?"*

This was an England sharply divided by the class system, in which the upper classes lived in luxury on the labour of the masses, whose lives were harsh and hungry. Justice did not favour the common man, who could be hanged or snatched from his family and transported for quite trivial offences. After the storming of the Bastille in France in 1789, there were those who contemplated rebellion in England too. But, by the grace of God, a movement was about to be born which would provide them with an alternative.

The Founders

In his history of the Primitive Methodist Church, Holliday Bickerstaff Kendall quotes the Rev. T Scrimshaw:

'That the power-loom, spinning-jenny, steam engine and the Primitive Methodist revival are in time closely related is not a mere coincidence. At a grave crisis in the industrial and domestic life of the nation Primitive Methodism was instituted.'[x]

The crises facing the nation at the time of the birth of Primitive Methodism affected practically every aspect of national and domestic life. The Napoleonic wars raged in Europe causing the ports to be closed, blocking the importation of food and the export of manufactured goods. Changes in industry towards greater mechanisation led to unemployment, hunger and the Luddite rebellion. The King was mad; George III was believed by his contemporaries to suffer from fits of insanity, though modern research indicates that he suffered from a rare blood disorder called porphyria, which was made significantly worse by arsenic in the medication he was given to treat it. The majority of his people were illiterate, the education of the poor being of little consequence or interest to those in a position to influence it. Though many thousands had been reached with the Gospel by John Wesley and his followers in the previous century, whole swathes of the country remained in ignorance, particularly in the rural areas. 'The masses in rural England were outside the churches and largely uncared for. Whole villages were without any resemblance of religious life.'[xi]

The people of the area around Hepworth were nominally members of the parish church of Kirkburton. When they died, long trains of grieving relatives wound their way over field and down lane, carrying the coffin on a cart or in turn on their shoulders the seven miles to the parish church. Many members of Gatehead were still buried in their family graves at Kirkburton even after the chapel was built. When they married or had their children christened, the long walk to the parish church was undertaken once again, but it is uncertain what other influence it held on their lives at that time.

Figure 3. Kirkburton Parish Church

The Established Church in the early years of the nineteenth century was, generally speaking, far from what it should have been. It collected taxes and perfunctorily hatched, matched and dispatched its parishioners but had little concern for their spiritual or even physical welfare or for the salvation of their souls. As Paul Cook remarks:

'The condition of the Anglican Church at the end of the eighteenth century and into the nineteenth was dire, best summed up by the ugly word latitudinarian, with most of the clergy given over to place-seeking, worldly pleasures and pursuits, together with a general neglect of spiritual duties'.[xii]

Mr Collins, the obsequious, self-seeking clergyman in Jane Austen's *Pride and Prejudice*, published in 1812, springs at once to mind. With her renowned perception, Jane Austen encapsulated the church of her society in the person of Mr Collins, with his undue deference to perceived social superiors and preoccupation with his own social standing.

Neither was this the finest hour of the Methodist Church. The British ruling classes lived in fear that the recent revolution in France would be re-enacted upon their own shores by the hungry, unemployed and disenfranchised poor. In its efforts to prove its loyalty to the establishment and maintain its aura of respectability, the Wesleyan leadership distanced itself from any concept of reform or empowerment of the working classes.

But there were some within the Methodist Connexion who were concerned with the plight of the masses. In the year 1800 a carpenter by the name of Hugh Bourne found himself working in Harrisehead in Staffordshire. The newly converted Bourne was horrified by the lives of the people of that district. 'Harrisehead had no means of grace and its inhabitants, chiefly colliers, appeared to be entirely destitute of religion and much addicted to ungodliness. It was indeed reckoned a profane neighbourhood above most others.'[xiii] 'Cock-fighting, bull-baiting, pugilism, drunkenness, blasphemy, all kinds of uncleanness, ferocity and crime, characterised the locality.'[xiv]

Hugh Bourne felt himself compelled to address the moral and spiritual condition of his neighbours. A conversation with his kinsman, Daniel Shubotham, on Christmas Day 1800, resulted not only in Daniel's conversion but in a style of evangelism which became known as 'conversation-preaching', which the painfully

15

shy Bourne undoubtedly preferred to public speaking. These two men, together with a collier called Matthias Bayley, were greatly used by God in the vicinity of Harrisehead. 'A work of religion, usually called a 'revival', took place . . . and there was great reformation in the neighbourhood.'[xv] One of those converted in this revival was William Clowes, who had returned to his home in Staffordshire after narrowly escaping the press gang in Hull. His rapid progress in the Christian life was such that Hugh Bourne prayed on one occasion, "Oh God, that Thou wouldst make me like him!"[xvi]

Figure 4. Hugh Bourne and William Clowes

Soon Hugh Bourne became a class leader and was subsequently prevailed upon to preach. On the occasion of his first sermon, so many people turned up that the house appointed for the service was too small to hold them and Bourne was compelled to preach in the open air. His love of outdoor worship was born there and culminated in the camp meetings which came to characterise the Primitive Methodist movement. Reports from America at that time of religious services held in the open air and continuing for several days were published in the Wesleyan

Magazine. These came to be known as camp meetings, no doubt because people came to them from great distances and camped during the night in the fields where the services were held. Already accustomed to worshipping in the open, Hugh Bourne's congregation enthusiastically embraced this idea and on 31st May 1807 the first camp meeting was held at Mow Cop on the Cheshire/Staffordshire border. Bourne himself was convinced that this type of service would be 'effective in reaching the class that had seemed unreachable by the ordinary agencies.'[xvii]

The Methodist Connexion, however, disapproved of the camp meeting and demanded that the practice be abandoned. When they refused, Bourne and Clowes were expelled from the Wesleyan Methodist society. Others left with them and in 1812 a meeting was held at which plans and regulations for the future conduct of a new society were discussed. It was at this meeting that James Crawfoot suggested the name 'Primitive Methodists' and the camp-meeting Methodists became a distinct denomination with a new name which underlined their enthusiasm for returning to the primitive zeal of John Wesley's travelling ministry.

The first Primitive Methodist circuit was formed at Tunstall, where a chapel was built in 1811, and others soon followed, thanks to the work of travelling preachers, such as Robert Key, John Oxtoby and, of course, Hugh Bourne and William Clowes. They were met frequently in the early days with persecution, the Establishment and the Established Church combining forces against them. They 'aroused in the parson and the squire something akin to dismay, followed by an angry determination to keep them out by fair means or foul.'[xviii] They were often dragged from the walls and benches which they used as pulpits and many were thrown into jail. Their often noisy style of preaching earned them the name 'ranters' but, by 1824, the Primitive Methodist Connexion had over 33,500 members. And it was in this year that one of its travelling preachers spoke to a meeting near Hepworth that would lead to the foundation of Gatehead Chapel.

John Hinchliffe was born in December 1766 at Clayton West in the West Riding of Yorkshire and was baptised at the parish church of Hoyland on the Hill or Hoylandswaine. His parents were devout Wesleyan Methodists, who provided hospitality to many travelling preachers, including John Wesley himself during his journeys through the Huddersfield area.[xix] It appears from subsequent events that in his youth, John Hinchliffe shared their faith.

On 26th December 1787, he married Martha Goldthorpe of Penistone.[xx] The young couple moved to Langsett, near Penistone, where John soon established a successful business as a wool manufacturer and trader. He purchased raw wool, which he dyed at home and then distributed to neighbouring houses to be spun and woven. The finished cloth was carried by pack horse to Staffordshire to be sold and, with the proceeds, John would purchase crockery from the Staffordshire potteries to be brought back and sold in Huddersfield.[xxi]

Figure 5. Sheep on Langsett Moor

18

Despite his financial success, however, John's spiritual life declined. His wife was not a Christian and there was no easily accessible centre of worship in the area. The neighbours among whom he lived and worked had little interest in matters of faith and John was some distance away from the example and counsel of his parents.

One day, Martha arranged what to modern ears seems a very harmless evening of entertainment. She invited their neighbours into her house to spend some pleasant time together and during the course of the evening, asked one of her guests to sing a song. For John, however, this was a step too far. Memories of his Methodist upbringing flooded back to him and he stood up at once to protest.

"No, Martha," he said. "I have been brought up in a pious family and song singing is not what I have been accustomed to. It is merely to please the devil and I will not have it."[xxii]

Martha responded indignantly that she was as likely to go to heaven as anyone else and more-so than most! But something had stirred in John's heart and he was adamant.

"We must repent of our sins and pray to God for forgiveness or else we shall go to hell," he said.[xxiii]

His deep sincerity touched Martha and both of them in the coming weeks sought a new relationship with God. Both came under a great sense of conviction and resolved to serve the Lord with all their might from that time forward. The nearest place of worship to their house was three miles distant, but they were notable for their regular attendance at Sunday services. In addition, John established a prayer meeting in his own neighbourhood and later a class meeting, both of which were successful and increased in both the number and piety of their attenders.

He had, however, according to his grandson, some peculiar opinions. Writing in about 1898 from Grimsby, where he was a shop keeper, Abel Hinchliffe stated:

'I may as well say here that my Grandfather was looked upon as a somewhat strange and outrageous character, as he was a religious Republican. He also strongly held that it was impossible for the millennium to come so long as people had to give all their time and strength in order to procure the bare necessities of life. There were not many asylums in those days or no doubt he might have been provided with lodgings there'.[xxiv]

Abel Hinchliffe was undoubtedly echoing views he had heard expressed by others, as he was only a boy of thirteen when his grandfather died. Nevertheless, John's conviction that people should have sufficient leisure time to pursue occupations other than work, especially perhaps religious instruction, may have been behind the great falling out with his neighbours that took place around 1807.

The cloth produced in the Penistone district had a good reputation and a spinning wheel could be found in almost every house in the area. So when John Hinchliffe, anxious to increase the amount of cloth produced, heard of a firm in Leeds which had produced a machine that would do the work of many spindles and produce a superior yarn in the process, he made haste to test it. Greatly impressed with its performance, he bought one and bought it back to Langsett. But he had severely misjudged the reaction of his neighbours. Far from being pleased at the prospect of more leisure time, they saw the end of their livelihoods looming. As Abel Hinchliffe wrote:

'Previous to getting the spinning machine, he was a popular man in the parish. . . but his introduction of a machine which in actual practice would do the work of thirty old machines fairly took their breath away and roused the women folk to defend themselves against the introduction of machinery that evidently meant starvation to them all.'[xxv]

Such was the furious reaction of the people of Langsett that John had no alternative but to take himself, his family and his machine and leave the district. He settled in a quiet hamlet near to Hepworth called Barnside and started up his business again at Swan Bank Mill at Underbank. It is probable that, with his enthusiasm for the mechanisation of the cloth-making process, he would in any case have moved in due course to a more populous area. As Eileen Williams points out in her book, *Holmfirth, from forest to township*:

'By 1806 an increasing number of power driven looms and cropping frames were making their impact . . . to an extent which was to alter the whole structure of working class life. Manufacturers (clothiers who were beginning to assemble the processes of spinning, weaving and finishing into one unit) were building larger mills to contain the machines in large numbers, transferring their work people from their homes to the enclosed factory premises'.[xxvi]

Figure 6. John Hinchliffe's house at Barnside, a drawing by Harold Battye.

21

John continued in the Methodist church, probably joining Hepworth Methodist Chapel at Jackson Bridge, which opened in 1809. He was a class leader in the Sunday School for a total of twenty- seven years. He and Martha raised seven children, of whom one, his eldest son Joseph, became a local preacher before dying prematurely, leaving a young widow. Martha, too, lived for only a few years after the move to Barnside. She died in 1814 and two years later John married again to a student in his class.

His new wife, Ann, had been brought up in the Church of England, but joined the Methodists after sitting under the ministry of William Clowes. She became a highly regarded member of the church and a great support to the cause, paying the class money for several of the poorer members. After her marriage to John Hinchliffe on 2nd January 1816, she continued to help him in his work.

In 1824 a well known Primitive Methodist preacher came to Barnside, where he visited the house of John and Ann's neighbours. Jeremiah Gilbert had been sent from the Nottingham circuit to establish a mission in Sheffield about ten years after the Primitive Methodist connexion began at Mow Cop. He had preached in various places during his journey and had been imprisoned at Bolsover Round House for 'preaching abroad'.[xxvii] On 23rd May 1821, he was staying in Silkstone after leading a meeting there when eleven men and boys lost their lives in the Norcroft pit disaster. A chain pulling the corve full of miners to the surface broke, causing them to plummet some thirty-seven feet to their deaths, and Jeremiah had the sorrowful task of visiting the bereaved and bringing to them what comfort he could.[xxviii] In 1823 he became the first minister of Bradwell Primitive Methodist Church,[xxix] but his was primarily an itinerant ministry and his travels continued to take him the length and breadth of his circuit and beyond.

John had possibly encountered the teachings of the Primitive Methodists on his journeys into Staffordshire and so when Jeremiah Gilbert preached at his neighbour's house, he went next door to hear him. He was particularly impressed by the singing of hymns from the small hymn book and at the end of the service, John went to his wife and said, "The poor preacher has a long way to go and perhaps nothing to eat. I should like to give him his tea."[xxx]

Ann immediately went next door and invited the preacher to her home. During the course of the ensuing meal, Jeremiah read aloud several passages from his journal, which so affected both John and Ann that they warmed to the teachings of the Primitive Methodists and soon after decided to join their number, as did others in the neighbourhood. The new church met in a number of houses in the vicinity, including Oxlee, Upper Nab, Lower Nab and Milshaw,[xxxi] but on 19th November 1825, John rode on horseback to York where he was granted a licence to use his house at Barnside as a place of worship for 'Protestant dissenters'. Again, a class was formed and John appointed its leader and, as it went from strength to strength, in due course a second class began. Ann shone in these classes; her care for her neighbours, both for their physical and spiritual welfare, endeared her to all and she loved to offer hospitality to the visiting preachers, who, for many years, used her large kitchen as their meeting house.

As numbers increased, however, it became apparent that a larger and more appropriate venue would have to be found. John and a group of the leading members of the new church sought a suitable venue on which to build a chapel and in 1835 located a parcel of land in the area called Gate Head where the road from Hepworth to Penistone crossed the new Huddersfield to Sheffield turnpike road.

Sadly, Ann did not live to see the little church community housed in its new home. Her health began to fail as 1835 drew to a close

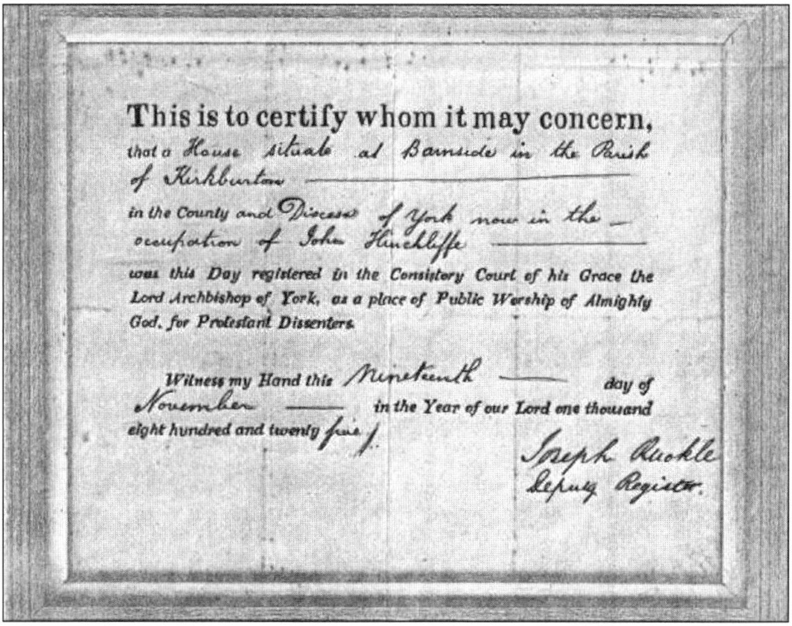

This is to certify whom it may concern,
that a House situate at Barnside in the Parish
of Kirkburton ————
in the County and Diocess of York now in the ——
occupation of John Hinchliffe ————
was this Day registered in the Consistory Court of his Grace the
Lord Archbishop of York, as a place of Public Worship of Almighty
God, for Protestant Dissenters.

Witness my Hand this *Nineteenth* ———— day of
November ———— in the Year of our Lord one thousand
eight hundred and twenty *five* /

Joseph Ruckle
Deputy Register.

Figure 7. The licence granted to John Hinchliffe,
which hangs in the vestry at Gatehead

and she spent much of her time confined to bed. By the following
Spring, she knew her days were numbered. Although, having
married at the age of forty-eight, she had no children of her
own, she had been a loving stepmother to John's children and
treasured them as though they were hers. They gathered around
her as she was dying and read to her passages from the Bible. At
one point she seemed to see the spirits of the dead children of
her stepdaughter, Martha, in the room. "What a quantity of little
children are round my bed. . .," she said, "and some of John
Beaumont's are among them."[xxxii] John and Martha Beaumont
had indeed lost several children in infancy and Ann's obituary
in the Primitive Methodist magazine noted with true Victorian
pathos, that it was 'no wonder these happy spirits hovered round
her dying bed, for she was a great lover of children and a spiritual
nursing mother to them'.[xxxiii]

Following Ann's death, John Hinchliffe suffered a stroke and was confined to his house for the remaining years of his life. A second stroke in 1841 deprived him of the use of all his limbs except for one arm, but he still found strength to say the Lord's Prayer and to listen to his daughter-in-law read to him from the Scriptures. He died early in 1841 and was buried in the graveyard of the Wesleyan Chapel at Jackson Bridge with his two wives. Their tombstone reads simply:

'Martha, wife of John Hinchliffe of Barnside, died March 3rd, 1814, aged 50 years. Ann, wife of the said John Hinchliff, died May 9th, 1836, aged 68 years. The said John Hinchliff, died February 19th, 1841, aged 74 years.'[xxxiv]

John Hinchliffe's will shows that, as well as his mill, he also owned property around Barnside and had mining interests in the colliery at Crow Edge, which he leased from the Earl of Scarbrough. These he left in equal shares to his two sons, John and Zaccheus, along with legacies of £300 each to his daughters: Mary, wife of John Battye, a farmer living at Daisy Lee[xxxv] in Hade Edge; Martha, wife of John Beaumont; and Sarah, wife of Timothy Crowther, a clothier of Hemsworth. He also provided for his daughter-in-law Martha, the wife of his dead son Joseph, and left a sum of money to his late wife's brother. But his spiritual legacy was a 'neat little chapel' on a hill, which despite his declining health, he saw through to its completion.

The Chapel

The land which John Hinchliffe and his colleagues selected for the building of the chapel had previously belonged to the Wentworth estate. It had been sold on the death of its owner to Mr William Heap, a manufacturer from Hepworth, but when he was declared bankrupt, it had been acquired by James Shaw, formerly of Lockwood.[xxxvi] The enclosure awards in 1834 state that:

'...we allot and award unto the said James Shaw of Hepworth all that allotment No. 149 containing two acres and four perches situate at Gate Head bounded eastward by Wadsley and Langsett road and Burnt Edge road westward by allotment herein awarded to John Marsh northward by Burnt Edge road and southward by old inclosures. And we order and direct that the said James Shaw and his heirs should make and maintain the fences of the said allotment against the roads'.[xxxvii]

A year later, the land was in the ownership of James's son, William. William Shaw was a wealthy man, listed in the 1851 census as a 'woollen mill proprietor, employing 9 men and 14 children at the mill and coal dealer employing 12 men and 13 children as miners and hurriers'. A list of collieries in a geological survey[xxxviii] taken in 1866 shows that he was by then the owner of the colliery at Barnside.

Obtaining land on which to build dissenting churches was frequently no easy task. In many localities, most of the land belonged to one person and though the squire and Church of England minister may have been unsuccessful in keeping the 'ranters' out of their villages, their combined forces could often ensure that no land was available for the building of their churches. Many congregations met for years in cottages, barns and other even less suitable buildings until a site could be identified and the money raised to build a chapel. But how those chapels were loved by the people who had scrimped and saved to build them!

On occasion, however, landowners may not have been entirely to blame. Joseph Ritson in his book *The Romance of Primitive Methodism*,[xxxix] published to mark the centenary of the Connexion in 1910, tells the amusing story of Willie Wilkinson, a sturdy, straight-talking dalesman. The congregation of Bowlees near Middleton-in-Teesdale had sent many requests to the landowner for a piece of land, but had received no response until Willie decided to take matters into his own hands. Having a shrewd idea that the landowner, the Duke of Cleveland, might not have actually received their requests, he presented himself at a local inn where he knew the Duke to be staying with a shooting party. He was refused admission but, being of a size and disposition not to be denied, brushed past the servant and marched into the Duke's presence. Grasping his hand in ebullient greeting, he began,

"Hoo aire ye, Mister Deuk, an' hoo's Missus Deuk?"

As the Duke of Cleveland was a man with faultless manners, as well as a sense of humour, Willie was welcomed and asked what brought him there that day.

"Ah want a bit o' grund, Mister Deuk, to beeld a Primitive Methodist cheppel on," he said. "Ah've sent pepper efter pepper myself an' nivver gitten ony word back."

The Duke's unfortunate agent, who happened to be present, was forced to admit to the truth of these allegations, justifying himself on the grounds that he had not deemed the matter of sufficient importance with which to trouble his Grace. His Grace, however, immediately granted Willie's request and ordered his agent to meet Willie at nine the following morning to stake out the agreed plot. Willie retired gratified, muttering in the direction of the hapless agent, "Ah olways thowt it was them nasty bodies aboot ye" and promising to convert a few poachers for the Duke.

Gatehead, however, seems to have enjoyed a consistently favourable relationship with local landowners. In 1835, William Shaw leased the plot of land to the congregation at a token rent, allowing its members to concentrate their efforts on raising money for the building fund. His brother and partner, Edward Shaw, became one of the chapel's first trustees. Harold Battye, a later trustee of the chapel, in his booklet celebrating its 150th anniversary, surmises that it cost a little over £100 to build, being slightly smaller than the chapel at Hade Edge, which cost £160. [xl] The average wage for a miner at that time was around sixteen shillings a week, but John Hinchliffe and his family were of more substantial means and contributed significantly to the cost. Everyone contributed, including even the young son of John and Mary Lindley of Upper Milshaw. James Lindley saved his pennies and contributed the first five shillings he ever possessed to the fund[xli], thereby demonstrating at an early age a love for the house of God at Gatehead, which was to last throughout his life.

The site which they chose looks at first glance an unlikely situation for a chapel. It is a thousand feet above sea level and there are few houses or indeed buildings of any kind in the vicinity even in the present day. A casual visitor might well wonder where this isolated little church found its congregation. But its position on the turnpike road from Huddersfield to Sheffield meant that access for visiting preachers from these towns was greatly eased, while the old road from Barnside to Penistone provided access for local people. With the coming of the railway, a daily horse-drawn coach service ran from Holmfirth, through New Mill to the train station at Hazlehead, passing right by the field in which the chapel was built. But most importantly, the visitor standing at the chapel can see the farmsteads of all its founding members:

Figure 8. The present-day chapel, showing its remote location

the Charlesworths of Upper Nab, the Hinchliffes of Barnside, the Lindleys of Milshaw and the Hirsts of Ox Lee. And as they worked on their farms during the week, or returned to them from mine or mill, these families would have been able to look up and see the little chapel on the hill, the focus of their spiritual and social lives. In the early days before the chapel was built, they had crossed the valley to each other's houses for Sunday worship and the story goes that they decided to build at the high point where their paths crossed, where the two roads meet at Gatehead.

The original chapel building was small and plain. It possessed none of the architectural merits or extravagances of many church buildings of a later period, but was built of stone to withstand the strong winds which blew from the moors and accommodated about one hundred worshippers. A schoolroom was built beneath the main church, little better than a cellar but which served both as a Sunday School and as a day school until Hepworth Council School opened in 1884.[xlii] William Shaw donated a sundial, which was placed on the south side of the chapel and bore the inscription *Nos et umbra* – 'we are as a shadow'. The schoolroom was heated by a small fireplace in the corner and the chapel by a stove near to the pulpit. Both were lit by candles and in the early days of the chapel's existence evening services continued to be held in the homes of worshippers in order to save money on heat and lighting. Mrs Moorhouse of Oxlee, Jonas Charlesworth of Upper Nab, John Hinchliffe of Barnside, George Hirst of Lower Nab, Adam Hirst of Oxlee, and John Lindley of Upper Milshaw all rendered hospitality to their neighbours in this regard.

Figure 9. The original chapel, opened in 1836,
from a drawing by Harold Battye

In 1838 the land upon which the chapel was built was formally conveyed to its trustees, each of whom paid the nominal sum of five shillings to William Shaw. The first trustees were Zaccheus Hinchliffe, clothier, of Barnside; John Hinchliffe, his brother, clothier, of Scholes; John Lindley, farmer, of Upper Milshaw; George Hirst, clothier, of Lower Milshaw; Jonas Charlesworth, farmer, of Upper Nab; George Heppenstall, stone mason; Edward Shaw, clothier; Thomas Booth, coal miner of Lower Nab; Abel Kaye, clothier, of Bird's Nest; William Oldham, clothier, of Barnside; Anthony Hirst, farmer, of Hepshaw; Adam Hirst, of Oxlee; George Bennett, coal miner, of Law; and Jonathan Holmes, coal miner, of Foster Place. The original trust deed states that they:

'Contracted with the said Wm. Shaw for the purchase of the plot of land hereinafter described and intended to be hereby conveyed for the price of three pounds and entered into contract in order to the building of a Chapel or meeting house upon the said plot of land for the use of a society or community of religious persons known as Primitive Methodists belonging to the Primitive Methodist Connexion and for the more particular use and accommodation of the members of such a connexion at and in the neighbourhood of Barnside and who have since erected and completed such a Chapel or meeting house and have nominated and elected Trustees for the said Chapel, in whom the same to be vested.'[xliii]

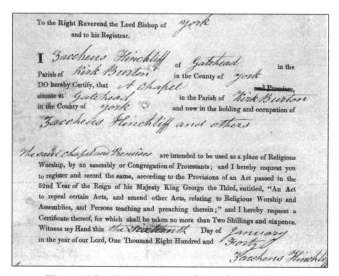

Figure 10. Registration of Gatehead Chapel

31

Zaccheus Hinchliffe submitted an application to the Archbishop of York, dated 16th January 1840, for the chapel at Gatehead to be registered as a place of worship for an 'assembly or Congregation of Protestants.'xliv A few year later, he himself had moved to Bullhouse where, along with his coal- mining interests, he is listed in the 1851 census as a farmer.

The census of religious worship taken in 1851 shows that, on the morning of 30th March of that year, nineteen people attended the service at Gatehead and ninety-one children went to Sunday School. In the afternoon, fifty-two people attended worship and there was no evening service that day. The entry was submitted by James Charlesworth, farmer and local preacher. However, Richard Ebenezer Leach, the curate of Holy Trinity Church in Holmfirth, notes in his submission that Sunday 30th March 1851 was an unfortunate date on which to take the survey as it was the day of the Holmfirth Fair, when attendance at divine service was traditionally low. Instead, people would dress in their Sunday best and walk into Holmfirth to see the fair and the processions. Mr Leach also notes that on this occasion it was raining! Numbers therefore may have been even higher on other Sundays.

Figure 11. The congregation in about 1950

The services held in the new chapel were quite different in tone from those of later years. Many people were unable to read or write and their knowledge of God was not one learned but one experienced and expressed with a depth of joy and zeal unknown to many of subsequent generations. Paul Cook describes the character of the people brought to faith in the revivals of the period:

'These simple, believing men and women looked for the wonderful works of God among them. They believed that unless God worked they were powerless to achieve anything in his name. This explains why they prayed so much and with such great earnestness. . . In their zeal they witnessed spontaneously to the saving power of Jesus Christ, and visited the homes of their neighbours with warm desire to see them enter into the same spiritual blessings.'[xlv]

Sermons, usually delivered by local preachers, were long but were devoid of abstract theology and full of emotion. They were received eagerly by their listeners and frequently interrupted by cries of 'Hallelujah, praise the Lord!' These preachers, farmers, weavers or miners by weekday, uttered the convictions of their hearts with evangelistic fervour and their words were heard with heart-felt joy. What they lacked in eloquence, they made up for in exuberance. The singing of the hymns was embraced equally joyfully. As many of the congregation could not read, the hymns were learned by heart and a 'liner' recited each line of the hymn before it was sung. Hymns also served to teach the truths of the Gospel to those who were unable to read the Bible for themselves and so were a particularly important part of worship. The Reverend Joel Mallinson, historian of the Methodist cause in the Holme Valley, noted: 'in singing, Wesleyan theology was largely learnt and new converts built up on the faith.'[xlvi] In those early days, Jonas Charlesworth of Upper Nab led the singing and founded Gatehead's first choir. They were accompanied by his brother, George, of Barnside, on the violin. If no musician was available, Joshua Lindley of Birds Nest or his neighbour George Kaye of Haystacks could be relied upon to strike up a tune. Later, a bass fiddle (or double bass) was purchased by subscription and this was used by Matthew Moorhouse to accompany the hymns until 1872, when a harmonium was purchased and Robinson Hirst became the chapel's first organist.[xlvii]

Figure 12. Playing the bass fiddle

Gatehead joined the new Huddersfield Primitive Methodist circuit that had been formed in 1824 with Thomas Holliday as its first superintendent. The minister was based at the Northumberland Street Primitive Methodist Church in Huddersfield and on the occasions when he rode out to take services at Gatehead, he was accommodated for the night at the home of John Hinchliffe, junior, who had returned from Scholes to the family home at Barnside following his father's death. When, in about 1862, a Chapel House was built to accommodate a caretaker, a bed was provided for visiting preachers and ministers there. The Chapel House was built over the flags laid outside the Sunday School room and the school was extended underneath it. The first caretaker to take up residence in the house was Tom Mellor, but his arrival caused severe disruption for a time. His whole family contracted scarlet fever, a much more serious illness then than it is today, and the school had to be closed for six weeks until the threat of infection had passed. Oil lamps also replaced candles to light the church at around this time and these improvements appear to have incurred a debt, as mention is made in a list of new trustees of a sum of money owing to a George Battye.[xlxiii]

The new trustees, appointed in 1868, were Jonas Charlesworth, Joseph Bardsley, William George England, George Battye, John Hirst, George Kaye, Amos Kaye, Aaron Heppenstall, Joseph Kaye, Adam Hirst, Joshua Lindley, John Lindley, Henry Noble and Isaac Hirst. This new generation decided that Gatehead should join the new Scholes Primitive Methodist circuit, which was formed in 1878. The other churches in the new circuit included Honley Southgate, Wooldale Town End and Scholes Methodist Church. A close fellowship developed between these churches, which in the case of Scholes continues to the present day.

The first minister of the new circuit was the Rev. Gregory, who, true to the maxim that Methodism was born in song, began singing classes at Gatehead, as a result of which a regular choir was formed. The voices of its members flowed out over the surrounding hills under the conductorship of Emmanuel

Charlesworth, the son of Jonas of Upper Nab, who remained as choir master until 1925. Music has continued to be a very important part of the life of Gatehead ever since.

Figure 13. A time capsule was placed under the cornerstone

The Rev. Isaiah Potts took over the role of circuit minister in 1886, by which time numbers had grown so significantly at Gatehead that it was considered imperative to expand the chapel. Further land was purchased from Sam Shaw, son of William Shaw by his second wife Ann, for the token price of five pounds and plans were drawn up to extend the chapel by twenty feet and six inches. A porch was built on the side and a vestry added to the building. Work had already commenced when on Saturday 31st July 1886, a stone-laying ceremony took place. Members of the congregation and friends of the chapel met at 3pm and walked up the hill to Victoria, where they met the Crow Edge Band coming the other way. The procession then returned to the chapel, where a Mr J Smith performed the stone-laying ceremony. A time capsule was carefully hidden under the stone, a glass bottle containing copies of local and national newspapers, the Scholes circuit plan and two coins of the realm. The celebration then continued with one of the public teas that played such an important part in the social life of the chapel, followed by a well attended talk in the evening.

Figure 14. Gatehead Chapel in 1886, after the extensions were completed, from a drawing by Harold Battye.

The work proceeded at such a pace that the reopening ceremony was able to take place on Saturday 16th October of the same year. Another tea was held in the schoolroom, followed again by a talk, and the reopening service was held the following day. The next Saturday saw one of the many bazaars which were held at Gatehead over the years in order to raise funds for the chapel. Though most of the people were far from wealthy, they gave generously to the cause and in 1891 were able to extend the vestry so that a young men's class could take place there on Sunday afternoons. Central heating was installed the same year. More coffee suppers and bazaars followed and in 1896 an organ was installed in the chapel at a cost of £148. This was a cause for great celebration, including a special service on 10th April at which all the choirs of the Scholes circuit sang and Edgar Battye played for the first time. A hand-loom weaver by day, he was to serve as organist at Gatehead for several years. The occasion made a marked impression on one young woman, Hannah Kaye, who remembered all her life the tone of the organ as it played the hymn, 'Lead kindly light', before the congregation set out through the dark lanes to return to their homes.[xlix] Harold Battye recalls that the organ was blown by hand. Two boys were paid the princely sum of ten shillings (50p) each per year to pump wind into the bellows and certainly earned their money during the Hallelujah Chorus!

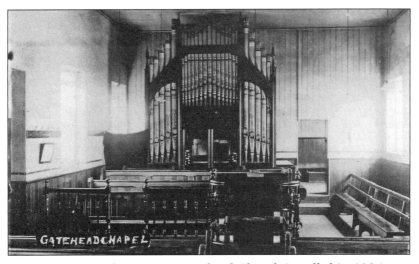

Figure 15. The organ at Gatehead Chapel, installed in 1896

Electricity was installed in the chapel in 1902, thanks to the generosity of Charles Shaw Tinker of Meal Hill, who allowed the chapel to be connected to his own private supply, a privilege which was still being enjoyed in 1936 when it celebrated its centenary. Gatehead thus became the first chapel in the district to have electric light. A solitary street light outside the chapel was lit from the same source and although the local council footed the bill for this, it was the responsibility of the caretaker at Gatehead to switch this light on each evening at lighting up time.[1]

The congregation now had a chapel such as they had prayed for and dreamed about. They had founded, in Harold Battye's words, a 'light on a hill'[li] to witness to the truths of the Gospel to future generations.

The People

In his history of Methodism in the Holme valley, Joel Mallinson gives a wonderful description of the character of the valley's inhabitants. He pays tribute to their independent spirit and deep convictions, and is struck by the fact that the geographical features of the landscape are reflected in the characteristics of the people who live there.

'The bold range of undulating hills, the wild moorlands, the sweep of country with cornfields, pastures and woods, and the deep wide valleys, contribute to build up a robust physique and sturdy manner, as trees give colour to the insects that live on their leaves and as water imparts its hue to the fish which disport therein. The curt speech and gruff manner are compatible with kindly feeling and a generous soul. No misunderstanding arose and no offence taken where it was never intended.'[lii]

Settlements at Barnside, Millshaw, Oxlee, Nab and Law, among others, had been in existence since the fifteenth century and some even before that. Whereas in the present day these farmsteads are inhabited in most cases by single families, in earlier times several families lived at each location and the members of these families married into each other, so that over time everyone in the close- knit community was related in some way. Everyone was someone else's aunt or cousin and the practice of giving the mother's maiden name as the Christian name of the eldest son shows in many cases the way in which these relationships evolved.

Mining, weaving and quarrying were the main occupations of the men and women who attended Gatehead Chapel and were the occupations of the children too. Many families combined these occupations with farming in order to provide for themselves and to barter for goods and services they needed. Families would rise before dawn to begin the working day, and the click of the hand looms in the upper rooms of weavers' houses kept time with the tap of wooden clogs on the cobbles, as mill and mine workers set out for the factories and pits. In the winter months, the smell of tallow candles permeated the houses as weavers continued working, frequently until nine in the evening.

Figure 16. Everyone in the close-knit community
was someone's aunt or cousin

There were several coal mines around Gatehead, mostly of the shallow drift-mine variety, in which workers walked in to the coal face directly from the hillside. Uriah Tinker of Meal Hill owned among others the colliery nearest to the chapel, known as Gatehead Bottom, as well as the brick works at Hepworth and the mine at Hepshaw.[liii] Hepworth Iron Works was another of the major employers in the area. Coal became an increasingly necessary commodity as the Industrial Revolution progressed, but very low wages were paid to the men who gave their lives to hewing it from the ground, and even lower wages to the children who worked alongside them. While the men hacked the coal from the coal face, it was the task of the children to deliver the corves of coal to the shaft entrance, either by pulling them or by pushing with their heads against the wooden tubs. Frequently, the children would be left to continue filling the corves with the day's hewn coal after the men had left.

William Shaw, giving evidence to the 1842 Royal Commission into the employment of children in the mines, stated that the youngest children working in the Foster Place Colliery, where he worked at that time as an agent, were nine or ten years of age and that there were no girls among them, although girls were certainly working in other pits in the district. Several of them were children whose families attended Gatehead Chapel. These children began work at seven or eight in the morning and continued until between three and five in the afternoon, sometimes longer. They hurried on average thirty-two scoops of coal each day, weighing two and a half tons each. William Shaw believed that restricting the number of hours worked would injure the working classes in the district, a reference no doubt to the loss of income which would result. Rachel Tinker of Meal Hill, aged thirteen and working at Uriah Tinker's pit, defended the use of female labour in the mines for the same reason. Her father, she said, had six daughters and no sons and 'we would be fast [stuck] if he could not send us to the pit'.[liv] All of the girls interviewed stated that they wore male clothing in the mines. A belt around their waists was fastened to a chain which went through their legs and attached to the corve and the chains frequently caused large tears in their breeches. Mary Holmes, daughter of Jonathan and Ann, modestly maintained that this never happened to her, but her story was contradicted by Ebenezer Healey of Foster Place, who testified with puerile glee as to her predicament in this regard that very day.[lv] In the introduction to his report, Jelinger C Symons, the commissioner gathering evidence in the West Riding of Yorkshire, abhors the employment of girls underground, principally for this reason, and Mary Holmes comes particularly to his attention:

'In one [pit], near New Mills, the chain, passing high up between the legs of two of these girls had worn large holes in their trousers and any sight more disgustingly indecent or revolting can scarcely be imagined than these girls at work. No brothel can beat it. I took their evidence afterwards when they were sent to me washed and dressed and one of them at least, was evidently crammed with her evidence.'[lvi]

The fact that almost every child denied that anyone had told them what to say lends credence to that very possibility. It is also noticeable that none of these children under the age of fourteen years is listed on the 1841 census as having an occupation. Both boys and girls stated that they were thrashed but maintained that it was frequently the older children who would thrash the younger ones rather than any punishment meted out by an overseer and indeed close family relationships may have fostered care for young trappers and hurriers. Several physicians were interviewed by Jelinger C Symons, and provided evidence of the consequences of working underground on the physical development of the children. Many had stunted growth, either from deformities caused by the work or from the prevalence of rickets. Asthma and respiratory problems were common, caused by the wet conditions in which the children and indeed the adults worked. Symons, describing Uriah Tinker's Day Hole Pit at Meal Hill, states that 'many of the gates are very wet, in some places water stands two inches, and the rails are in bad repair. The children, girls as well as boys, go on all fours with belt and chain, a younger one thrusting sometimes behind.'[lvii] Accidents were frequent, from falls or burns in particular. However, while Symons observes that a collier at the age of fifty was an aged man, he regards the 'broad stalwart frame' of the miner as infinitely preferable to that of the ' puny, pallid, starveling little weaver with his dirty white apron and his feminine look'![lviii]

People lived in houses built of local stone, generally having two or three and occasionally four rooms. It was not uncommon for more than one family to occupy a house and in particular for married children to share accommodation with their parents and younger siblings. In smaller dwellings, this might result in the whole family sleeping in one room or the children sleeping in the upstairs room while their parents made up a bed downstairs. Wealthier weavers might have a shut-up bed, which was pulled down at night but during the day had the appearance of an attractive chest of drawers. Sharing beds was common and privacy was a commodity hard to come by. In weavers' cottages, beds were frequently in the same upstairs room that housed the hand looms and children might sleep within the frame of the loom itself if space was limited, as space for the loom took precedence. Room for a lodger might also be required, to bring in extra income and to provide accommodation for workers travelling from other districts for employment.

Figure 17. A family from Gatehead, their names now lost

The houses had flagged floors, sprinkled with sand and covered with pieces of hessian from old corn sacks. Sand trapped the dirt walked into houses from the unmade roads outside and made the floors easier to sweep clean. The women made rag rugs from pieces of spare cloth and hessian begged from the mills. A rug-making frame would be brought out or borrowed and friends and family would gather to help peg the strips of cloth through the hessian backing. These were happy occasions when stories were passed down from one generation to another. The rugs were kept upstairs during the working week and brought down for use on a Sunday and on other special occasions.[lix] The walls inside the houses were whitewashed and the doorsteps donkey-stoned. Whitsun was the time for new clothes or for old ones to be washed and mended and made fit to serve for another year. At Easter, the August Feast and Christmas, the houses were 'spring-cleaned' and beds and blankets washed and hung in the fresh air to dry. Floors were swept with 'besoms' or brooms. In the 1841 census, besom-making was a frequent occupation of Hepworth folk, including women, who would gather bunches of heather from the moors and tie them onto a simple handle to make brooms either for their own domestic use or to sell in the markets.

In the production of food, the country people around Gatehead were undoubtedly more fortunate than their town- and city-dwelling contemporaries. Oatmeal was their staple food and farmers would tread their home-grown oatmeal down into large oak chests, wearing white socks kept for the purpose and packing it so tightly that they could cut out portions without disturbing the rest when they wanted to use it.[lx] The principal purpose for which oatmeal was used was in making porridge which was the usual food consumed at breakfast and often at other meals of the day. Nettle porridge, while sounding most unappetising to modern ears, was undoubtedly very nutritious. Oats were also used in the production of oat cakes, another staple food, which were baked on hot stone slabs or hotplates in the cottage kitchens and then hung up on the 'bread reel' to dry out. Bread was of a much coarser consistency that its modern equivalent and oat bread was less highly valued than the more refined wheat bread.

Country people benefited from the fruit and vegetables that they could grow in their gardens and most families had a 'potato piece' in which to grow this other staple food. Many people kept a pig which would be slaughtered in the autumn and its meat preserved to feed the family over the winter. As meat was expensive, many people would have none once this source was exhausted. When questioned about her diet, Betty Swallow of Oxlee, aged eleven, told the 1842 Commission that she returned home from the mine to 'sometimes meat pie and sometimes potatoes. Sometimes nothing but potatoes.'[lxi] While at work in the mine, she would have had a slice of bread to sustain her, perhaps with some bacon fat, or some oatcake, which she would have eaten underground.

Many of the women brewed their own beer and one of the tasks of their children was to walk to the brewery at Shepley to fetch yeast. Possibly this was the brewery which Seth Senior founded in 1829, reputedly with a borrowed sovereign[lxii]. The Sovereign Inn which now stands on the site was named in honour of the story. The children took with them small cans into which yeast was scooped from the top of the vats for the sum of one penny. The yeast would then be carried home and used on both brewing and baking days.

Wild fruits growing in the hedgerows were a valuable addition to the diet but unexpected dangers could be encountered in obtaining them. James N Kaye, who for many years tended the graveyard at Gatehead, tells of an incident which happened to his grandfather as a boy of eight in 1835:

'At that time and up until a few years ago, there used to be a good crop of bilberries on Cheesegate Nab. On this particular day, my grandfather, James Kaye, had gone bilberrying on Cheesegate Nab. He had a two quart piggin [wooden pail] with him. He had got it full when he heard someone in the direction of Meal Hill give a whistle and a shout but he ignored it and went on bilberrying. The next thing he saw was a man on a galloping horse racing towards him. He ran off as fast as his legs would carry him but was caught up before he could get onto Dick Edge Lane. This person lashed him with his riding whip and he was forced to let go of his piggin of bilberries. The horseman then made his horse rear up and it trampled and smashed both the piggin and the bilberries flat. The person in question was Uriah Tinker of Meal Hill.'[lxiii]

Uriah Tinker, local mine, mill and land owner, was something of a character. In 1844, he built a tower, known locally as Tinker's Monument, which became a well known local landmark until its deteriorating condition caused it to collapse during a thunder storm. But despite his idiosyncrasies, his descendants were loyal friends and benefactors of the little chapel at Gatehead.

People generally worked six days a week. Being unable to work and provide for a family was greatly feared, as there was no social-welfare network to fall back on. For this reason, most wage earners became members of one or another of the 'sick clubs' or friendly societies, such as the United Ancient Order of Druids, which came to prevalence in Victorian England. Each member paid a small amount each week into a central fund which was used to support a member too sick to work or, if necessary, pay for his funeral. There were no set holidays, though the pits and mills would be closed for a couple of days over Christmas, and the local feasts and church anniversaries were much anticipated and well attended. As the miners determined their own hours of work and were paid accordingly, the day after pay day would sometimes see few of them in the pits and a half- day holiday would sometimes be declared.[lxiv] But for one group of men, the

Sabbath was not a day for resting. As D F E Sykes declared:

'It would perhaps be no little exaggeration to say that Methodism owes as much to its non-commissioned officers or lay preachers, commonly called local preachers, as to its ministers duly ordained. Often of limited education, generally of limited means, but of unlimited fervour and devotion, these men have sown the good seed broadcast with a profuse hand. After working at the loom or counter for six hard days during the week, they are more than content, they exult, to make their way to distant missions and in little Bethels on the moorside their sonorous voices may still be heard Sunday after Sunday, raised high, very high, in song and prayer and exposition.'[lxv]

Figure 18. Some of the members of Gatehead Chapel c.1912
Joe Driver, Tom Marsh, Hubert Beever, Charles William Charlesworth,
C Kaye, C W Moorehouse, B Lindley, G Bamforth, G Kaye
Florence Maude, Sarah Kaye, C Shaw, Emmanuel Charlesworth,
A Kaye, A Heppenstall, E Wagstaffe, F Robinson, N Maude
M Lindley, M H Charlesworth, M Charlesworth, E A Kaye,
E Heppenstall, H Wagstaffe, E Turner

Gatehead Chapel was the spiritual home of many such local preachers and at one time supplied more than half the lay preachers in the Scholes Circuit. In the early days, Jonas Charlesworth of Upper Nab and Abel Kaye of Birds Nest, both founding trustees of the chapel, travelled to churches and meetings as far away as Battyeford near Mirfield; sometimes on horseback and sometimes on foot. Others included Joshua Lindley senior and Henry Lindley, James Woodcock, Matthew Moorhouse, Luke Turton, Joseph Shaw and C W Kaye. Some went from Gatehead into the ministry. The Rev. Hezekiah Cook was a scholar in the Sunday School, as was the Rev. John Kaye who later emigrated to America.

Not everyone's life was immediately influenced for the good by attendance at the chapel. In March 1887, the Huddersfield Chronicle[lxvi] reported on a case at Holmfirth Petty Sessions in which two young women, on their way to a service at Gatehead Chapel on the Sunday evening two weeks previously, had come to blows. One had apparently accused the other of stealing a silk handkerchief and in the ensuing fracas had her tooth knocked out. She retaliated by hitting her accuser over the head with her umbrella. A young man named Brook Robinson, who witnessed the altercation, told the court that the two girls were both as bad as each other and the magistrates apparently agreed as they imposed a fine of ten shillings rather than the maximum possible sentence of two months imprisonment.

Straying animals appeared to be a frequent problem, according to the newspapers of the time. In October 1890, two Hepworth farmers, Eli Brook and Mary Ann Wagstaffe, were each fined two shillings and sixpence for allowing cows to stray onto the highway at Gatehead.[lxvii] And in 1885, Joah Swallow, a joiner from New Mill, was fined the same amount for leaving his mule and cart unattended on the highway. Unfortunately for him, they were discovered outside Gatehead Farm by Police Constable Haynes who, after waiting ten minutes to see if anyone turned up, led the animal back up the road to the Victoria Inn. Sure enough, there he found Joah Swallow.[lxviii]

The Lindley family of Hepworth was intimately associated with Gatehead Chapel throughout its history. The earliest memories of the first generation of children were of the Primitive Methodist missionaries holding services in the house of their parents, John and Mary, at Milshaw. Several of their descendants were themselves called as a result into the ministry. John, the eldest son of Joshua Lindley senior, was sent by the Clayton West Circuit to the Theological Institute in Sunderland but was rejected by virtue of the fact that he did not 'give reason of persons converted under his labours'. It was necessary at that time to show proof of calling by enumerating the people converted under one's ministry and although John appealed against the decision and was later offered a place, he appears not to have taken it up. It was left to his younger brother to take up the calling and the Rev. Joshua Lindley can be tracked in the censuses travelling the length of the country as a Primitive Methodist minister, who expressed his 'very decided views and forceful convictions. . . in strong, sometimes rugged, language'.[lxix] He died in 1950 at the age of ninety-three.

Ezra Lindley, son of the young boy who saved his pennies to contribute to the building of Gatehead Chapel, was called to preach at an extraordinarily young age. He worked underground as a trapper and later as a miner and was convicted of his sin while still of tender years. Together with his brothers, he was instrumental in commencing a Primitive Methodist Sunday School in Thurlstone, where his ability soon became apparent:

'He became a Sunday School teacher and evinced an aptitude to teach of no mean order; he displayed peculiar talents for the exposition of the word of God and in all his movements he manifested unusual marks of intelligence and abilities which the authorities of the station were not slow to observe. Hence he was called out by the December Quarterly Meeting in 1864 at the age of 14 years to labour as a local preacher in the Clayton West circuit. His endeavours ... met with great success, being blest to the edification of God's people.'[lxx]

However, Ezra's ministry was to be short lived. At the age of nineteen, he developed an abscess on his leg which baffled his doctors and refused to heal. After long spells in Huddersfield Royal Infirmary, often in great pain, he died at the age of twenty-two and was buried at Netherfield Independent Chapel in Penistone. Three years later, his heartbroken father James was buried in the same grave.

Nor was this the only tragedy to befall the Lindley family. John and Hannah Lindley farmed at Drake Hill, near Cumberworth. On the morning of 1st August 1887, Hannah and her son Herbert, aged twelve, were attending to the milking when they saw a fox terrier which they did not recognise enter their yard. The dog was obviously suffering from rabies and it attacked Herbert, biting him on the hand. Hearing his brother's cries, Fred Lindley, who was washing himself indoors, came running out to assist and was also bitten. The family's dog chased off the intruder but the Lindleys subsequently discovered that it had bitten a third man, John William Whiteley. All three were treated by Dr Laxton of Shepley who decided to take them to Paris for treatment by the famous chemist and biologist, Louis Pasteur.

Rabies was on the increase in Europe and Louis Pasteur, following his success in the field of vaccination against life threatening ailments, had turned his attention to the prevention of this dreaded disease. Most patients suffering from infection by the rabies virus at that time died a painful death from hydrophobia but two years earlier, in 1885, Pasteur had successfully treated a young boy, Joseph Meister, with a series of vaccinations. Since then, rabies patients from all over Europe had been brought to him and, in August 1887, Fred and Herbert Lindley joined their number.

At first, the treatment appeared to have been successful. But on 4th October that year, the Holmfirth Express carried the following story:

'Fred Lindley of Hepworth, one of the three people bitten by a mad dog on August 1st, died from hydrophobia. After being bitten, he and two other injured people had been taken to Paris for a fortnightly treatment under M. Pasteur and had returned home seemingly none the worse for having been bitten. It was not until some time after that the symptoms of hydrophobia revealed themselves.'

Fred was buried in the little cemetery in front of Gatehead Chapel. Five years later, his brother Herbert joined him in the family grave. The dog which had tried to protect them was shot.[lxxi]

Figure 19. Family grave of Fred and Herbert Lindley in Gatehead churchyard

In the early days of Primitive Methodism, the pit villages, centres at that time of barbarity and drunkenness, were consistently missioned by the travelling preachers, who spoke at first in the open air and subsequently established their little chapels, changing the moral tone of the villages for the better. As they trained local preachers to minister to these chapels, they instilled in them a love and understanding of law, order, freedom and democracy and they taught them how to articulate these concepts in their preaching. By so doing, they unwittingly equipped them not only as preachers but also as leaders in the burgeoning trade-union movement. For as the Primitive Methodist Church entrusted a larger share of its governance to laymen than any other church in the country, so it increased their suitability as leaders of the miners and other workers in their struggles for social and political improvements. As Joseph Ritson put it:

'While in no sense a political church, it prepared men for the intelligent discussion of political questions and gave them the instincts which must constitute the foundation of a wise and stable democracy.'[lxxii]

Ernest Beever, who together with his brother Hubert was one of Gatehead's trustees, was one such individual. He was the branch delegate of the National Union of Mineworkers, representing the Gatehead Branch and in 1926, during the Miners' Strike, travelled to London with some delegates from Barnsley at the request of Winston Churchill to meet him at the House of Commons. Unsurprisingly, he returned saying that the trip had been a waste of time and money.[lxxiii] However, both Ernest and Hubert went on to be elected as councillors on the old New Mill Council before its amalgamation with Holmfirth Urban District Council, representing the Scholes and Fulstone wards respectively. Both were chairmen of the Council during the 1950s.[lxxiv] And both had spent their formative years as pupils in the Sunday School at Gatehead.

The Sunday School

At the beginning of the nineteenth century, few people were interested in the education of the working class. A fear of the revolutionary spirit prevalent in Europe reinforced the conservative viewpoint of the upper classes, whose priorities consisted in economic development, the creation of wealth and the maintenance of the status quo. The majority of the workers themselves had no use for education, being reluctant to give up the wage-earning capacity of their children. But as the century progressed, attitudes began to change. Instances of crime and rioting increased among people who were penniless and starving and at the same time, the commercial and manufacturing supremacy of Great Britain was in decline, as other European countries had more developed technical education systems. Educating the workers began to be considered as financially viable.

In 1838 the Huskar Pit disaster in Silkstone, near Barnsley, in which twenty-six children between the ages of nine and sixteen drowned, raised public awareness of the conditions in which children worked underground. Queen Victoria revealed her feelings by sending condolences to the families. This gave added impetus and support to the inquiry into conditions in the mines initiated by Lord Ashley (later the Earl of Shaftesbury). The subsequent Mines Act of 1842 prohibited the employment underground of all females and boys under the age of ten. The Factory Acts of 1833, 1844 and 1867 also imposed restrictions on child labour and the possibility of educating working- class children began to gain feasibility.

Sunday schools had been around in one form or another since the sixteenth century. In 1801, there were 2,290 Sunday schools but by 1851 this number had grown to 23,135[lxxv] and most children attended Sunday school, whether or not their parents attended church. The original purpose of these schools was the education of working-class children in reading and writing rather than in the truths of Scripture, although as the Bible was used as the text book for literacy lessons, it was hoped that they would also come to understand the basis of their faith. This proved not always to be the case!

The worshippers at the new chapel at Gatehead were determined from the outset that their children, both boys and girls, would benefit from education. The first tiny school room was built at the same time as the chapel itself and parents went to great lengths to ensure that their offspring attended. In the days of voluminous skirts in female apparel, Adam Hirst of Oxlee walked ahead of his daughters, Hannah, Ann, Jane and Martha, across the fields to the chapel, dragging a branch behind him to knock droplets of water from the long grass and keep them as dry as possible.[lxxvi]

Figure 20. Cousins Joyce Battye and Patricia Robinson formed a life-long attachment to Gatehead Chapel

55

Though there had been a school in Hepworth since 1649, with an endowment given by a Mr Philip Bray to cover the costs of educating four children from poor families, few others had the means to enable their children to attend. In the report of the 1842 Commission on the employment of children in the mines, Jelinger C Symons noted that, 'their wages are not sufficient to enable the colliers to give their children education and they earnestly desire to have better means of education'.[lxxvii] Several children from the Gatehead area, including some whose parents attended the chapel and who could therefore be assumed to attend Gatehead's Sunday school, were interviewed by the commissioners and their answers give a startling insight into their standard of education as well as their religious understanding. 'With regard to the fruits of education and with respect even to the common truths of Christianity and facts of Scripture, I am confident that the majority are in a state of Heathen ignorance', opined Symons.[lxxviii]

Isaac Hirst, the thirteen-year-old son of the above Adam Hirst, one of Gatehead's first trustees, was examined by the commissioners at Low Moor, Hepworth, on 15th June 1841. He testified that he went to Sunday school, where he could read the New Testament and have it explained to him. "Christ came to save sinners," he said. "Sinners is us."[lxxix] Betty, eleven-year-old daughter of Jeremiah Swallow of Oxlee, said the same, adding that she said her prayers every night.

Brothers Henry and Ebenezer Heeley of Foster Place, however, also went to Sunday school and claimed to be able to read a little but they appeared not to understand what they had read. Henry, aged eleven, knew that God made the world and that He had a Son. However, he could not say who the Son was. "I read about John and Luke and Matthew in the Testament but not about Christ. I know nothing about Him." Ebenezer, at thirteen, did not know who Jesus Christ was either, though he had heard about Him being nailed to a cross.

Henry Cartwright aged twelve, had never been to Sunday school, did not know his letters and had never been taught to pray. He knew that God had made the world and had heard of Jesus Christ, "but I don't know who He was or whether He was Church or Chapel". And Caroline Swallow, at the age of eight and a half, declared that she had given over going to school. Jellinger Symons notes caustically in the margin of his report, 'she knows nothing.'

Jellinger Symons believed that the reason behind the inability of children to give reasoned answers despite school attendance lay in the fact that they were instructed to learn by rote, rather than being taught to reason and comprehend:

'The notion is invetcrately implanted in the mind of the great majority of the schoolmasters and schoolmistresses, that comprehension is no necessary part of instruction and others seem to imagine it a matter of intuition and are astonished that a child has not learned what it has never had the means of understanding. "Have I not been preaching justification by faith, by the law of Moses, and setting forth the essence of the Godhead, this very morning?" exclaimed a Calvinist preacher and schoolmaster in a paroxysm of amazement of finding that a group of scholars could not explain who or what Christ was! The chances against a child are very great, first, there are the chances that the teacher does not, or cannot, put himself in the position of a child, to feel its ignorances and supply them, [then] there is the chance that where apt instruction is given the child's attention is not gained, and which the elliptical system of questioning is so admirably adapted to secure. It therefore follows that in the vast majority of cases child and teacher jog on in the established ruts, so ingeniously devised to avoid the exercise of mind and everything in the shape of instruction, save the mere mechanism of memory.'[lxxx]

Sunday schools were nevertheless credited with major steps

forward in the moral education of young people. In his history of the village of Meltham, six miles from Gatehead, the Rev. Joseph Hughes notes that:

'A beneficial change has taken place in the tone of society throughout the whole kingdom .... and is perhaps nowhere more strongly marked than in the West Riding of Yorkshire. This is doubtless mainly attributable to the humanising influence of Sabbath schools, to which the district of Meltham, in common with many others, owes much of its advance in civilisation and morals'.[lxxxi]

Figure 21. Charles Kaye and sons Albert and Arthur taking children on a Sunday School trip around 1920

Many of the children themselves expressed a desire to learn, seeing in education a way out of the mills and mines, and the numbers attending Gatehead Sunday school steadily increased. As time passed and more children came, a day school was also opened and continued until the opening of Hepworth Council

School in 1884, after primary education became compulsory in 1880. Gatehead's day-school children then transferred to this school, which continues to the present day as Hepworth Junior and Infants. From this time onwards, Sunday schools concerned themselves only with religious instruction.

Will Battye, Joseph Bardsley, Jonas Charlesworth and Jabez Bunting were the schoolmasters at Gatehead between the years 1836 and 1884 when the school closed.[lxxxii] At first the children were taught reading, writing and accounts and later Mrs Bunting taught the girls knitting and sewing. Some children walked many miles to attend, bringing their lunches with them during the harsh weather of winter so that they would also be able to stay for the afternoon session.

The roof of the schoolroom sloped downwards, as the pews in the chapel above sloped upwards, so that at the far end of the room standing was extremely difficult. Iron pillars supported the roof. Over time, candles were replaced by oil lamps hung on the walls to provide light and the fireplace in the corner gave way to a coke burner in the centre of the room, around which the children clustered to warm themselves before the service on cold Sunday mornings. Sometimes too they were allowed to roast nuts and make popcorn on it. Seats were fixed around the walls and, when these were full, wooden forms were arranged in the centre of the room. These could be neatly stacked out of the way when space was needed for teas, dances and other entertainments. When the organ was installed in the chapel in 1896, the harmonium was transferred down to the schoolroom but by this time its bellows leaked and it had to be pedalled furiously in order to put out a tune.[lxxxiii]

Processions, or parades, of one sort or another, featured prominently in the life of the Sunday school from its earliest days. In 1856 a grand parade took place in Holmfirth to proclaim and celebrate the peace at the end of the Crimean War and the

Huddersfield Chronicle records that Gatehead School was one of many that took part.[lxxxiv] Church bells rang and flags flew from shops and houses as, at noon, the procession consisting of some six to seven thousand people began its progression, on foot, wagon and horseback, from the Town Hall and through the district. At Wooldale, villagers had built a triumphal arch, decorated with evergreens and bearing the message 'Welcome, ye Messengers of Peace'. From there, the procession wound its way through Totties, Scholes Moor, Cross, Underbank, Lane End and back to the Town Hall. While a hearty meal was provided for the elderly residents (that is, those over 60!) in Victoria Street, the children were dismissed back to their various Sunday schools, where they partook of a treat of tea and currant buns. Tea and currant buns came to be an integral part of any celebration at Gatehead.

The Huddersfield Chronicle also recorded that, 'every Sunday school was provided with a banner, inscribed with the name of the school. The majority of these were really splendid.'[lxxxv] It was most probably this banner which was from then on carried at the head of the procession on Sunday school feast days. It was so large that it required six men to carry it but its use continued until about 1920, when it was ripped apart by the powerful winds that buffet Gatehead and had to be replaced with something easier to handle. A blue banner with gold tassels was acquired, decorated with a beautifully painted picture of an angel watching over a small child as it chased a butterfly near to a cliff edge.

Sunday school feasts were celebrated as local holidays by children and adults alike. Following their banner, and preceded by the Crow Edge Brass Band, they would walk in procession from the school, through Barnside and Hepworth, stopping at various points to sing hymns and then returning to the school room for a tea.

Figure 22. Following the band on a Sunday school parade

In the early days of the chapel's history, when the school room was too small to accommodate the numbers attending, a tent was erected by a high wall that had been built behind the chapel. The direction of the wind determined on which side of the wall the tent would be positioned. Its use continued until 1862 when, arriving to dismantle the tent on the morning after the feast, the men of Gatehead found it ripped to shreds. On this occasion, it was not the wind that constantly batters the chapel that was to blame but a group of late night revellers who had taken refuge there. But by the following year the schoolroom had been extended and tea could be enjoyed indoors. Harold Battye recalls that water for the tea was collected from Brow Well, half way down the steep hill to Barnside, by the caretaker at the time, George Bamford.[lxxxvi] Normally, water was collected from Bar Well and was delivered in tubs on a trolley, which could be heard rattling down the hill to the chapel before any celebration. But Mr Bamford insisted that only the water from Brow Well was good enough for making tea and he collected it personally in two cans slung on a yoke across his shoulders. The water was boiled in a tin boiler over the fire and the tea brewed in a wash tub, kept especially for the purpose by a Mrs Hirst. There was no crockery at the chapel, so the children brought their own mugs, while cups and saucers were borrowed from houses in the vicinity for the adults. While the adults sat down to a fork tea, the children ate their currant buns and Sunday school cake perched on the lower pews in the chapel before trooping back down the hill to Barnside. There, in the evening, a gala was held in one of the fields, with music from the band, games for the children and gossip for the adults. Many people with links to Gatehead made a point of returning to the chapel for Sunday school feasts and many family reunions took place there.

Figure 23. Sunday school feast at Gatehead

On one occasion, though, tragedy struck. On a Sunday school feast day in the 1880s, two farmers in Barnside were trying out a new horse-drawn mowing machine when something spooked the horses and they bolted. One of the farmers fell under the blades of the mower and both his feet were severed. He died before he reached hospital. After that, the date of the Sunday school feast was brought forward a couple of weeks, so as not to fall on the anniversary of this tragic event.[lxxxvii]

Each August another procession would wend its way around the district. The tradition of camp meetings which so characterised the Primitive Methodist movement was honoured by Gatehead Chapel each year with a camp meeting on Woodroyd Hill. On the morning of the meeting, the Sunday school scholars, their teachers and the preachers who were due to speak would progress up the hill to Victoria and on up to Woodroyd Hill, and would 'bid', or invite, people to accompany them. Then, as at the birth of the movement, the purpose of camp meetings was to attract people who would not normally attend church and reach them with the Gospel.

Figure 24. Camp meeting on Woodroyd Hill
(drawing by Harold Battye)

A team of preachers took the services, standing on farm wagons to speak in turn to the crowd assembled on the hill. Local men Luke Turton and James Woodcock were regular preachers. At first the long-suffering harmonium was hoisted onto a wagon and taken along to accompany the hymns but in later years a small section of the Crow Edge Band provided the music. Christenings frequently took place at camp meetings, adding to the feeling of festivity. In the evening, after a day spent in the fresh air, the congregation would retire to the chapel for a 'love feast', a kind of sacrament come prayer meeting, at which seed cake and water were used instead of the traditional bread and wine.[lxxxviii]

Figure 25. Choir trips in 1920 and 1922

Figure 26. Annual missionary weekend in 1897

The chapel was the focal point of the social as well as the religious life of the community and social events were also held there, especially those aimed at fund-raising for its improvement and expansion. Bazaars were a favoured means of doing this and were frequently held at strategic times in the chapel's history. Concerts were also popular and often followed a tea or coffee evening. Groups from within the church membership gave performances – the choir, the married ladies, the young people, for example – and local 'celebrities' often provided an added impetus for people to attend. The school room was completely unsuitable for such events and so a platform was erected in the chapel for the performers and each event had a chairman, or master of ceremonies, who sat in the pulpit. Additional seats, which rose in steps, were erected at the back for the children and the smallest boys were allowed to sit at the very top. They were thrilled at being able to look down onto the heads of the audience and could also peer over into the organ and see the pipes and sound boxes working, as well as the accumulated dust from years of use.

Fred Booth was the chairman in February 1897, when the annual missionary meeting was treated to the thrilling account of the Rev. Harvey Roe who, along with his wife, Annie, was shipwrecked off the coast of Africa while on his way to Fernando Po as a missionary. Their ship, the SS Corsico, struck a rock and sank during a storm off the coast of Guinea. They managed to get into a lifeboat and with the help of a friendly native reached the shore, where they were fortunate enough to be cared for by two Dutch merchants from the firm of Hendrik Muller in Rotterdam. They spent ten days living in a little wooden house in the jungle before being picked up by the steamer Benguela and eventually making it back to Liverpool.[lxxxix]

No doubt the small boys on the top row would have listened spellbound to the tale. Sadly, some of them were of an age where their own coming adventure would not end so happily.

The Wars

The early years of the twentieth century saw the Primitive Methodists planning celebrations for the centenary of their movement. Camp meetings were held on Mow Cop in 1907 and 1910, the numbers in attendance provoking the Daily Mail headline 'Sixty Thousand Methodists on a Mountain'.[xc] Services of thanksgiving were held, praising God for 'the grace and blessing so richly bestowed upon us during the hundred years of our history'.[xci] And mindful of its origins, the Primitive Methodist Conference for the year 1907 declared:

'This Conference is of one mind in its grateful recollection of the men whose names are inscribed high on the Church's Roll, who served in exalted positions, the great administrators and ecclesiastical statesman who inspired and shaped the Connexion's policy in the past; but not less gratefully does it cherish the memory of the nameless host, who in town and village, in quietness and obscurity, served their day and generation, making society sweeter by their labours, and who looked for no reward on earth.'[xcii]

Figure 27. Beautifully illustrated copies of the 1907 Conference resolution were widely distributed.

The 'abounding hope'[xciii] with which the conference looked forward to the new century was, however, severely tested in the days and months following. The movement which had come to existence during the Napoleonic wars soon found itself commencing its centenary celebrations under the threat of the greatest war the world had yet known. Despite its leanings towards pacifism, the Primitive Methodist Connexion believed that the coming confrontation was just, and when war was declared many thousands of its young men left their towns and villages and joined up. Many thousands did not come back.

The wall of the present Gatehead chapel proudly but sadly displays a plaque in memory of two such young men. Fred Cartwright and Jonas Kaye were cousins, grandsons of Jonas Charlesworth of Upper Nab, who had been a founding trustee of the chapel and a zealous local preacher until his early death in 1868. In the old graveyard, a headstone tells of another soldier, Joseph Battye, who also did not return. All three died within weeks of each other in 1917.

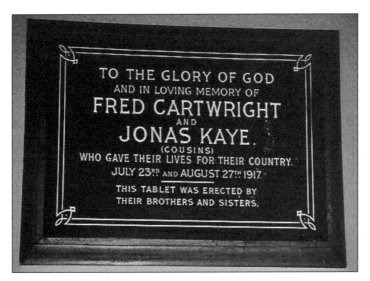

Figure 28. The plaque in memory of two cousins from Gatehead

Fred Cartwright had been born in New Mill in 1888 but by the time of the 1911 census, his parents, James and Hannah, had moved to Dogley Farm in Fenay Bridge and Fred was employed on the farm. James died one year after the move and Hannah must have watched in trepidation as Fred left to join up so soon afterwards. He enlisted in the Kings Own Yorkshire Light Infantry and was killed on 23rd July 1917. He is buried in the Ramscappelle Road Military Cemetery in Nieuwpoort, Belgium. Hannah died just two months after receiving the news of her son's death.

Jonas Kaye was the son of Hannah's elder sister Elizabeth and her husband George, both of whom had died prior to the outbreak of war. Jonas was the baby of the family and unmarried. Before the war he worked as a newsagent and tobacconist and lived near to his sister, Emma Bamford, in Doncaster. Aged twenty-nine, he enlisted in 1916 after conscription was introduced and was enrolled in the 6th Battalion of the York and Lancaster Regiment. He was killed on 27th August 1917, while serving as a stretcher bearer near the village of Langemark in Belgium. After the war, his sister Emma wrote a poignant letter to the commanding officer of the 6th Battalion in an attempt to find out what had happened to him. She had discovered through her own enquiries that the battalion's medical officer had been with Jonas at his death bed and hoped to trace this man to find out how Jonas had died. It is not recorded whether or not she was successful. Like so many other families, the Kayes may never have known how their brother met his fate. All they had left were his medals and personal effects that were sent to his sister Anice Cartwright in Skelmanthorpe. One identity disc, one letter and one fork are the only items still legible on the list of his effects.

For much of the war, the opposing German and Allied forces had been at a stalemate on the Western Front, on either side of a continuous line of trenches stretching from the coast of Belgium to the Swiss border.[xciv] From 1915 the Allied objective was to break through this line and engage the German army in the open French countryside beyond, where their superior numbers would give them the advantage. On 3rd May 1917 a second attempt was made by British forces of the Duke of Wellington's West Riding Regiment to penetrate the German line near the village of Bullecourt in France. Although they managed to push the Germans out of the village, they incurred heavy losses. Among them was Joseph Battye. Joseph was the second son of Jonas and Hannah Battye, who farmed at Whitley House Farm and later at Upperhouse. He is listed on the 1911 census as a plate fitter on the railway and when he was killed on the first day of the attack on Bullecourt, he was forty-one years of age. Though he had no known grave, the members, scholars and friends at Gatehead erected a memorial stone in loving memory of Joseph alongside his family tomb.

Altogether some fifteen thousand men who claimed membership of the Primitive Methodist Church perished in the Great War.[xcv] Their sacrifice was honoured at the Church's conference, held in 1918 at Northampton, by J. Tolefree Parr, who expressed his conviction, and hope, that, 'the truths taught them in the Sabbath School enabled them to meet death with calm assurance. They shared the faith of Rupert Brooke, the poet:

> *Safe where no safety is, safe though I fall;*
> *And if these poor limbs die, safest of all.*'[xcvi]

The horrors of this conflict had not faded from the minds of those who had survived when on Sunday 3rd September 1939, Neville Chamberlain's announcement confirmed that it would all begin again. Local people were taken by surprise when the air-raid sirens sounded for the first time during that same night and some thirty people from Jackson Bridge took refuge in a shaft at Wood Top Pit dressed only in their night clothes.[xcvii] Mine shafts appear often to have served as air-raid shelters for people living in rural areas. Gatehead member Doris Mary Wagstaff, who lived at Crow Edge at the time, remembers that she and her father once took shelter in Crow Edge Pit during a raid but that she refused to go down a second time. Both she and Margaret Sanderson can recall watching and hearing the bombs which fell on Sheffield in December 1940 as the German air force launched raids from northern France targeting the city's steel and armaments industries. Many hundreds were killed during the so called Sheffield Blitz and many thousands more injured or made homeless. King George VI and Queen Elizabeth toured the city in the aftermath, viewing the destruction and chatting to the crowds, bringing what words of comfort they could to those who had lost homes and loved ones. A couple of years later, two bombs fell on Crow Edge itself as a German bomber heading for Sheffield missed its target. Both exploded on the outskirts of the village but fortunately on this occasion no-one was injured.

The district's looms were put to work at full capacity, producing cloth for uniforms and silk for parachutes. By order of the police the mill sirens were to remain silent, unless needed to warn local people of an approaching air raid.[xcviii] Dobroyd's Mill at Jackson Bridge, which provided employment for many of the women and girls connected with Gatehead Chapel, began production of khaki. David Brown's in Meltham produced gears for Spitfires and Broadbents in Huddersfield made mini submarines.[xcix] When conscription began, men between the ages of eighteen and forty-one, not in restricted employment, were informed that they would be required to join one of the armed forces as their age bracket was called up. One in ten men were sent into the mines, becoming known as the Bevan Boys. In 1941 single women aged twenty to thirty were also conscripted, not to fight but to work in restricted occupations, particularly factories and farming, to free the men for active service. Children were evacuated to the area from Brighton, some finding life in Yorkshire so agreeable that they did not wish to return home at the end of the war.

Memories of the great flood of 1852 in Holmfirth haunted

members of its Urban District Council. Fearful of a recurrence of the tragic loss of life, which occurred when the Bilberry Dam burst, sending a torrent of water and debris crashing through the town, they made plans ' for the transfer, if necessary, of children of Holmfirth homes situated in the bottom of the valley, in the path of a flood consequent upon enemy attack, to other houses on the hillside, out of reach of the flood peril.'[c]

John Robinson, who later rose to become the manager of the post office in Holmfirth, was at the outbreak of the second World War just beginning work as a messenger boy. He walked for miles in all weathers along the lanes and across the fields around Holmfirth as he delivered telegrams, amassing an encyclopaedic knowledge of the area which he retains to the present day. On several occasions he had the sorrowful task of delivering a telegram which he knew to contain the worst of news. In most cases he also knew the serviceman concerned and the family whose lives were about to be shattered.

An indirect casualty of the war was Crow Edge Band. Many of those who made up its number marched off at the beginning of the war, some never to return, and those who survived had no heart for playing without them. The band had led the Sunday school and camp-meeting processions at Gatehead for the last time.

Those who remained behind at Gatehead Chapel during the war years sought to keep up the spirits of local people and visitors alike by continuing the round of dances, concerts and beetle drives[ci] which had been the focus of the chapel's social life for so many years. At least one wedding came about as a result. Mrs Mary Smith recalls that her young man became so disenchanted with having to walk her home from dances during the blackout, along the steep, pitch-black lanes leading from the chapel, that he decided that they had better get married.

Victory in Europe Day on 8th May 1945 marked the end of the war in Britain, though, of course, British troops were still engaged in the war against Japan. In Holmfirth, as elsewhere, the day was celebrated with a mixture of elation and sadness, as those who attended the street parties and church services remembered those who could not. The world would not be quite the same again and at the little chapel at Gatehead too, things were slowly changing.

The New Building

The numbers attending Sunday school in the years before the First World War made the requirement for new premises imperative. There had been a surplus of £12 remaining when the organ was installed and it was decided to use this to start a building fund to provide more suitable accommodation for the scholars. A bazaar was held in 1901, which raised £92 towards this objective. The total then gathered interest in the bank until 1910, when a second bazaar took place over the weekend of 26th - 28th March. A further £110 was raised, a significant start, in those days, to the building fund.

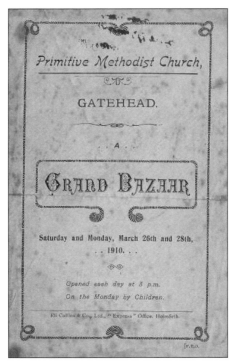

Figure 29. The bazaar in 1910 was held to raise funds for the new school

Two years later, in 1912, a plot of land was given to the trustees of the chapel by Sam Shaw. It was some 703 yards square and was situated on the opposite side of the road leading to Barnside. The church decided that at last building could commence. A substantial wall was built to surround the plot and toilet facilities were installed. But the coming war changed the focus of priorities and work on the Sunday school was suspended until more certain times.

New trustees were appointed in 1912: Joe Cartwright, Alfred Lindley, David Lindley, Norman Lindley, George Kaye, Luke Turton, Joseph Shaw and Charles William Charlesworth oversaw the life and work of the chapel during the remaining years of Primitive Methodism.

A decision was taken in 1925 to build the new Sunday school the following year but no building materialised. The money in the bank continued to gain interest, supplemented from time to time by further fund-raising events, until in 1931 the Sunday school teachers sent a letter of complaint to the trustees. Attempting to teach classes of children aged between five and fifteen in the same room was no easy task, they pointed out. A meeting of the congregation was called under the chairmanship of the Rev. J R Davies, and the question of whether to commence building was answered with a resounding affirmative. Designs were tendered by firms of local architects and that of Messrs Lunn and Kaye of Milnsbridge was chosen.

The building fund by this time stood at £540, a substantial sum at a time when the average weekly wage was about £2.50 but still only half the amount needed. In order to raise the remaining funds, a building committee was established, with Hubert Beever as its secretary and Emmanuel Charlesworth as treasurer. Due to their sterling efforts gifts and subscriptions came pouring in, ranging from a few shillings to fifty pounds, and testimony to the affection in which the chapel at Gatehead was held. So successful were their efforts that, despite the fact that the country was suffering under the Great Depression and many people had no employment, at the time of the stone- laying ceremony the trustees were confident that the building could be completed free from debt.

Figure 30. Edgar Battye lays a stone on behalf of the Sunday School

A subscription of £10 or more entitled the giver to lay one of the foundation stones of the new building and to have it inscribed, either with their own name or in memory of family members connected with the chapel who had passed away. The ceremony took place on Saturday, 3rd October 1931, with the Rev. J R Davies and the Rev. D J Bisbrown presiding. Fifteen stones were laid: seven by James Lindley, Albert Beever, Joseph Shaw, George Kaye, Joe Cartwright, T Shaw Tinker and on behalf of the teachers and scholars of the Sunday school, by Edgar Battye and Doris Kaye; and seven in memory of Jeremiah Womersley's family, Jonas Charlesworth, Mr and Mrs Kaye of Middlecliffe, Mr and Mrs James Cartwright, Amos Kaye, Mr and Mrs J Charlesworth of Upper Nab, Charles William Charlesworth and John Lindley and family of Drake Hill. Each person who had laid a stone was presented with an inscribed mallet as a memento of the occasion.

The ceremony was followed once again by tea in the old schoolroom and an evening entertainment in the chapel, with speakers, including the Rev. Bert W Tinkler, a former minister, the choir, conducted by Herman Kaye, and a soloist named Hilda Whipp. So successful was the occasion that several other members of the church decided that they would like to increase their subscriptions in order that they also would be eligible to lay a stone. Consequently another stone-laying ceremony was arranged shortly afterwards, at which stones were laid by Arthur Heppenstall and in memory of Robinson Cartwright, Mr and Mrs George Kaye of Barnside, Mr and Mrs Moorhouse, Mr and Mrs Swallow Charlesworth, Mr and Mrs Thomas Kaye and Mr and Mrs J Roebuck and family.

Building work continued throughout the winter months, a grim task as anyone who has experienced the rain around Gatehead, which blows sideways and soaks in minutes, will testify. But Mrs Bowden, the wife of the chapel's caretaker, looked after the workers, brewing them endless cups of hot tea and drying their wet clothes. And they were visited frequently by Mr Joe Alsop, a retired farmer and greengrocer from Hepworth with a flowing grey beard and a wealth of country lore at his fingertips, who provided them with the benefit of his insight into the coming weather conditions. Between them all, they succeeded in having the building ready for the opening ceremony on 12th March 1932.

Figure 31. The new school building in 1932,
from a drawing by Harold Battye

It was singularly appropriate that Sir James Peace Hinchliffe should open the new school building. Sir James was chairman of the West Riding County Council and his wide-ranging interests and knowledge made him an interesting and entertaining speaker. But more importantly, he was the great-grandson of the John Hinchliffe who, one hundred years previously, had ridden to York to register his kitchen at Barnside as the meeting place of the church's forebears.

In 1850 John's son, John Hinchliffe Junior, one of Gatehead Chapel's original trustees, had moved the family textile business to Denby Dale, acquiring Hartcliffe Mill next to the River Dearne. When he died in 1870, his son Zaccheus took over the business, which still trades as Z Hinchliffe and Sons in Denby Dale to this day. Zaccheus was succeeded in the family firm by his three sons, John, James Peace and Thomas Albert, each of whom made a significant contribution, not only to the business but also to the wider community in which they lived. In addition to his role as a managing director of the family firm, James Peace Hinchliffe served on the county council, where his belief that education was vital for the promotion of industry led him to chair a committee responsible for the provision of one hundred and fifty new schools.[cii] He served as a magistrate, championed the causes of demobilised soldiers during the First World War and chaired a committee, which housed and cared for over six thousand refugees before they were repatriated.[ciii] He was elected chairman of the County Council in 1916 and knighted in 1920.

Despite the many calls on his time, Sir James had remained faithful to the Methodist convictions of his predecessors, attending the Wesleyan church in Denby Dale, and was pleased to accept the invitation of the membership of Gatehead to open their new school. On Saturday, 12th March 1932, he returned to the chapel his ancestors had helped to build nearly a century before to perform the opening ceremony. The school was built of local stone and roofed with Welsh blue slate and consisted of a hall which would seat around one hundred persons and two classrooms. The building was centrally heated, a luxury after the cold of the old room under the chapel, but had no running water supply until 1958, after which 'the clatter of the trolley was heard no more'.[civ]

In his address to the packed hall, Sir James Hinchliffe spoke of the importance of the role of the Sunday schools. It was announced that the building had cost a total of £1,235 and that, not only had more than half of this sum, £677. 16s. 9d. to be exact, been raised by subscriptions, but the school had been opened free from debt and a surplus of £27 remained to be put into the school funds. Hubert Beever was presented by Luke Turton with a framed and inscribed photograph of the new school in appreciation of his achievement as secretary of the building fund in bringing this about. The celebrations continued into the evening with songs and speeches, including one from Joseph Shaw, one of the oldest members of the chapel, whose reminiscences of times past brought the chapel's history to life. The people of Gatehead felt on that occasion that they had achieved something worthy of celebration, that they had provided a legacy to be handed down to future generations and as the Huddersfield Examiner reported a few days later:

'Perhaps it is the air, perhaps it is because they still inherit the enthusiasm of their forefathers who founded the chapel, perhaps both, but the fact remains that a more devout and enthusiastic band of church workers would be impossible to find anywhere.'[cv]

Figure 32. Cleaning the new school building:
Mrs Elsworth, W. Bowden (caretaker), Mrs Moorhouse
Mrs Lindley, Mrs Bowden, Mrs Turner, Mrs E. Hirst

The year 1932 was a significant one for Gatehead Chapel. It marked the end of Primitive Methodism as a separate denomination when the Wesleyan, Primitive and United Methodists agreed to join together to form the Methodist Church of Great Britain. Known as the Methodist Union, the merging of the three strands of Methodism was celebrated in September of that year, its stated aim being 'the more effective evangelisation of the world and service of the age'.[cvi] The local Primitive Methodist chapels now joined the plan of the Huddersfield Circuit, although Gatehead still retained much of its Primitive Methodist way of doing things.

A new trust deed was executed in June 1932 and new trustees appointed to lead the church into the union. Ernest Beever, Sam Cartwright, Charles William Kaye, Norman Turner, Thomas Nichols, Herman H Kaye, Edgar Battye, James A Kaye, Hubert Beever and Arthur Marsh now served in this capacity.

James Lindley, son of Joshua Lindley Junior, died in 1932, shortly after laying one of the foundation stones for the new Sunday School. In his will he left the family farm at Drake Hill to Gatehead Methodist Church, stating that he wished it to be sold 'for the upkeep of the chapel and my father's grave'.[cvii] Opportunity soon arose to realise his request. The year 1936 saw the chapel's centenary and, as a means of celebrating the occasion, it was decided to refurbish the chapel completely.

Figure 33. Gatehead Chapel in 1936, with the new school on the right

81

Additional funding was raised by Gatehead's customary means of a bazaar, which, despite the rigorous fund-raising of just a few years previously, was a great success. It was opened by a Mr William Haigh and was followed by a pie and pea supper in the old schoolroom under the chapel, after which this room was closed up and never used again.

The chapel was redecorated throughout, new carpets were laid and cushions purchased and new and improved lighting was installed. The reopening ceremony was held, appropriately, at Easter, on 11th April 1936, and was performed by Miss Dora Lindley, niece of James Lindley whose bequest had made so much of the work possible. After a service in the chapel led by the Rev. Norman Povey, everyone crowded into the new schoolroom for a celebratory tea and in the evening a public meeting led by Mr Harry Dawson of Huddersfield provided an opportunity for reminiscing. There were those present on that occasion who could remember the chapel as it was originally before it had been extended, a small stone edifice standing firm against the wind and for the faith of its founders. Some had received their first taste of education in the old schoolroom below the chapel and had lived through astounding changes during their lifetimes. They felt sure that their achievements ensured the future of the chapel for another hundred years and the following Sunday held a service of thanksgiving, to give thanks and glory to God for all His blessings to them.

But the air of celebration was not to last for long. War clouds hung over Europe and broke three years later. When they lifted, church attendance declined once more, as it had after the first World War, although compared to many churches, Gatehead maintained the numbers in its congregation, as its children grew up and brought their own offspring to the family church.

When in 1947 the chapel's organist, Miss Jenny Marsh, became engaged to be married to Mr Cedric Battye, she decided that she wanted the ceremony to take place in the chapel where she served and worshipped. Since the original church had been built in 1836, no marriage had ever taken place within its walls but the Rev. Walter Pollard, Superintendent Minister of the Holmfirth Circuit, applied for the chapel to be licensed and had the pleasure of performing its very first marriage ceremony himself. The reception was held in the new schoolroom. Several of Jenny's friends followed her example and Gatehead Chapel has been privileged to witness many such happy occasions over the ensuing years.

The winter of 1947 was a particularly memorable one. The worst blizzards in Britain in the twentieth century saw snow drifting higher than human arms could reach. Electricity was limited to

Figure 34. Mrs May Booth in Farmer Lane in the snows of 1947

nineteen hours a day in domestic premises and food was rationed to levels not experienced even in the recent war, as animals died from the cold and vegetables remained frozen in the ground. [cviii] Tony Bacon, who lived at Victoria at the time, recalls that anyone from the locality who died during that winter had to be transported across the fields to the graveyard at Gatehead on a horse-drawn sledge. [cix]

By 1962 only five trustees remained. Norman Lindley, Sam Cartwright, Charles William Kaye and Ernest and Hubert Beever still served in this capacity but new hands were needed. John Arthur Holmes, Michael S England, Thomas E Grayson, Harold Robinson, Clifford Stanley, Harry Battye, Leslie Kaye and Harold Battye now joined their number. The congregation expanded too in 1969 when the chapels in Crowedge and Hepworth closed their doors for the last time and their remaining members were welcomed into fellowship at Gatehead. And, in 1979, they were joined by the last members of the chapel at Dunford Bridge when that too closed.

Nevertheless, as time went on, the congregation at Gatehead found it increasingly difficult to support the cost of maintaining two buildings. The caretaker's cottage was small, cramped and ill laid-out. It needed a major reconfiguration to make it suitable for modern living. Heating both the chapel and the school was prohibitively expensive and the vestry had been frequently used for the Sunday school, rather than the new building, in order to try to reduce costs. When the new Sunday school was occasionally used, the chill of disuse permeated people's bones. And then they examined the roof of the chapel. The oldest part of the building, erected by the chapel's founders nearly a century and a half previously from the materials available to them, was found to be supported by rough oak timbers, cut from the valley and untreated, which had over the years been riddled by woodworm. The time had come. A decision had to be made.

The trustees met on 3rd February 1971 and agreed on two resolutions to be put to the Church. Firstly, that in view of the constant difficulties encountered in maintaining two buildings, from henceforth all activities at Gatehead should be concentrated in one building. And secondly, that as the new school was the better building, it should be put in order, made suitably dignified for worship services and become the new home of the society at Gatehead.

On 26th February 1971 the Church met to consider their proposals. They agreed unequivocally that the Methodist witness at Gatehead should be continued. And with some reluctance, for they loved the old chapel that their ancestors had built and for which they had cared over so many years, they agreed that it should be sold and the money thus raised put towards the cost of transforming the school into a place of worship. They pledged whatever sums they could afford to defray the costs and decided to do the work themselves, creating their own place of worship as their forbears had done more than a hundred years previously.

Figure 35. Teas have always been a popular form of fund raising at Gatehead

85

The sale of the chapel was agreed at a price of £500 and work commenced. Throughout the spring and summer of that year, the congregation gave of their free time, their skills, their talents and their labour to transform a school into a church. Every person had a part to play and a contribution to make, so that when the work was completed they, like their forefathers, felt a deep connection to the work of their own hands. It proved impossible to transfer the organ; moving it would have been prohibitively expensive and anyway there was no room for it in the school building, so it was reluctantly sold and a small Hammond electric organ purchased in its stead. During the transformation, the time capsule buried under the cornerstone during the extensions of 1886 was recovered and incorporated into the wall of the new garden of rest, thus maintaining the link with the past.

Figure 36. In 2012 Mrs Pat England celebrated sixty years of playing the organ at Gatehead

At six in the evening of Saturday 18th September 1971, the Methodist society at Gatehead met in the old chapel for the last time. Rev. J Furbank commenced the service, giving thanks to God for the church and all who had passed through its doors over the years, saying,

"We enter our Father's house in the multitude of his mercies, in the wonder of His love and in the joy of His children's gratitude. Let us offer Him our thanksgiving and worship, assembled for the last time in this place.[cx]

The congregation then stood and in a symbolic gesture walked across the road to their new home, closing the door of the old chapel behind them for the last time.

Figure 37. Arriving at the old chapel for the last time

The Rev. Herbert Lindley, who had ministered in the Methodist cause for many years in Australia, performed the opening ceremony, speaking of his family's long association with Gatehead from its earliest days. Then the congregation filed into the newly converted church, where the Rev. F W Burton and the Rev. Furbank conducted the dedication service. A musical evening followed with tunes played for the first time on the new organ and Harold Battye was presented with a gold watch in appreciation of his hard work in organising the conversion. The evening concluded with refreshments and the little chapel began again in its new home, as its old one was converted into a private dwelling.

Eleven years later, 20th March 1982 marked the fiftieth anniversary of the new schoolroom, now the chapel. Another ceremony was held, opened this time by Fred Lindley of Harrogate and followed by speeches from representatives of the various sections of the church. A tea and concert were held in the evening and a commemorative plate was commissioned to mark the occasion. Later that year a traditional camp meeting was held once more at Upper Nab farm, former home of Jonas Charlesworth and still at that time the home of another member of Gatehead, Janey Armitage. Once again, the voices of the preachers and the music of the band rang out across the hillside.

Figure 38. Camp meeting at Upper Nab Farm

The Holmfirth Express ran several articles describing the history of Gatehead chapel when, in 1986, it celebrated its 150th anniversary. They were aided considerably by a commemorative booklet written by Harold Battye, who also produced the illustration for a mug commissioned to mark the occasion. Invitations were extended to anyone with links to the chapel to come to a reunion tea on Saturday 19th April and view an exhibition of photographs, documents and artefacts associated with the history of Gatehead. The time capsule was once again unearthed to form part of the display. A musical evening followed and the next day two thanksgiving services were led by the Rev. Fred Turner.

Figure 39. Jeffrey Turner conducts the band during an outdoor service to mark the 150th anniversary of Gatehead Chapel

Harold Battye had been a member of Gatehead all his life. His earliest memories were of being carried up the steep hill from Barnside to the Sunday school and he had served the church and members there ever since. When he retired from his business as a commissioned weaver in Birdwell, near Barnsley, he finally found time to concentrate on his favourite pastime. He had begun drawing in the trenches during World War II but now he attended the watercolour painting classes run by famous local artist Ashley Jackson, with whom he became firm friends. His talent for painting soon became apparent and he loved to walk the hills and villages around Gatehead seeking suitable views to capture. He painted hundreds and there are few members of the chapel today who do not treasure a picture that Harold painted for them of their home or a local place of personal significance.

Figure 40. Harold Battye

Harold never charged people for his paintings. He always gave them away as gifts to friends and family. And after his death in 1988, he gave one final gift to the chapel he had loved. During the weekend of 5th and 6th June 1993, all the friends to whom he had given paintings brought them back to the chapel and an exhibition of Harold's work was held to raise funds for the work at Gatehead. It was opened by Ashley Jackson and limited-edition prints were sold of the twelve Hepworth pictures, which provoked particular interest. Harold's nephew, Leslie Tinker, recalls sleeping on the floor of the chapel on the Saturday night, together with some of the younger men from Gatehead, to provide security. He later made a gift of the Hepworth pictures to the village, paying for them to be professionally framed and mounted. Four now hang in the village hall, four in the football club and four in the school.

Figure 41. Ashley Jackson signs autographs at the exhibition of Harold Battye's paintings

Two years later the funds were needed when major structural problems were discovered in the church roof. The original Welsh slate roof had withstood the winds for more than sixty years but now urgently needed replacing in order to prevent further damage occurring. Though they did not have the full sum required, the church officials decided to press ahead with re-roofing and send out an appeal to the friends of Gatehead and to local businesses for the rest of the finance. Once again, coffee mornings were held and bring-and-buy sales replaced the bazaars of Gatehead's past fund-raising efforts. The success of these endeavours and the generosity with which they were attended demonstrated the affection in which the little chapel on the hill was held. A month later, the local press reported that the congregation could once more make their way into chapel without negotiating piles of building materials as the new roof was complete.[cxi] Some damage had been done, however, to the internal decoration of the chapel and in 1996 it was redecorated and new curtains were hung. During this process, some of the original wall stencils from when the school was built in 1931 were uncovered.

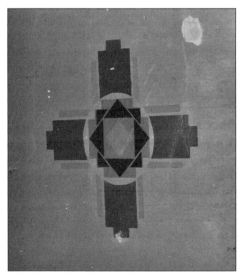

Figure 42. One of the original wall stencils

At the 150th anniversary in 1986, the Holmfirth Express quoted the Rev. Eric Forman, minister of Gatehead at the time, as saying, "I really believe that the chapel will be here in another 150 years."[cxii] Its editorial comment was, 'no doubt the Holme Valley Express will be running another feature in the year 2136, celebrating the 300th anniversary of the founding of Gatehead Methodist Chapel.'[cxiii] And at the conclusion of his booklet marking the event, Harold Battye had written,

'We look forward with confidence and in the sure knowledge that as God has helped and sustained us in the past, He will do so in the future, and we must spare no effort to ensure that the church at Gatehead continues to be a 'light on a hill' to witness to future generations'.[cxiv]

The church was financially secure and was deeply loved by many people. There was no reason to believe that these predictions would not come to pass.

Epilogue

A shepherd was faced with the task of persuading a sheep whose lamb had died to adopt a lamb that had lost its mother. He gently flayed the skin from the dead lamb and draped it across the orphan like a mantle, before putting it out in the fold with its adoptive mother. The sheep sniffed and licked the lamb very carefully, as if to ask, "do you really belong to me?" At last, the painstaking work of the shepherd was rewarded when the sheep accepted the lamb as its own. There is something of Christianity in this, thought the shepherd. Christ, in His death, puts our sins upon Himself so that we might be clothed in His righteousness and therefore be found acceptable to God.

This story was told in the local Methodist newsletter at Easter 1984 by the Rev. Brian Newbold, the minister of Gatehead at that time. For nearly two hundred years, the people of Gatehead had seen similar stories enacted all around them, as they watched the miracle of creation begin anew each Spring, witnessed God's provision for both man and beast in the fields and hedgerows and felt His love in the warmth of the sun on their faces. When they sang at harvest time of 'bringing in the sheaves', it was a task in which they had recently participated and they genuinely rejoiced that all was safely gathered in. When they read or heard the stories that Jesus told, illustrated with examples from the farming community in which He lived, they understood them with the benefit of personal experience and observation. The faith which grew from watching God at work was gentle, unassuming, and underlined by a quiet assurance.

They were also a self-reliant people. For generations they had supplied their own needs from the land around them and supplemented their incomes in mine and mill. When they needed a chapel, they had built their own, raising the money to pay for it, to extend it, and to care for it, themselves. While ministers had come and gone, the same families had worshipped in their chapel for generations and, even after the Methodist Union of 1932, the congregation at Gatehead obdurately insisted on doing things the way they had always done them.

Things were not, however, the way they had always been. In 1971, when the old chapel was used for the last time, Leslie Tinker videocd the congregation's procession into their new home. The film shows a crowd of people: children running between the gravestones; teenagers smiling shyly at the camera; adults of all ages chatting to each other. But Gatehead was not immune to the changes affecting the rest of society. Despite the fact that most people in Britain completing census forms still consider themselves to be Christian, church-going over the past few decades has become the exception rather than the norm. People now opt in to church, rather than opting out and church groups are moving from asking "'will our children have faith?" to "will our faith have children?"'[cxv]

Over the years, the numbers attending weekly services at Gatehead have dropped and, for the first time, generation has not followed generation into the fold. The chapel is no longer the focus of the social life of the surrounding area. Dances, pantomimes, beetle drives and many other forms of entertainment once held there have gone out of fashion and people look elsewhere for their sources of diversion. There are fewer local preachers and those who remain are offering to take fewer services, as many themselves advance in years. The numbers entering the ministry have fallen and fewer ministers are stretched between greater numbers of churches, having consequently less time for the pastoral oversight of each. At one time circuit churches ran themselves, the members taking responsibility for their ministries and administration, while the minister visited once a month to administer the sacrament. With the decline in numbers this is increasingly impracticable and churches are having to consider whether their futures are sustainable. Once again mergers are being considered on both a local and a national level and questions asked as to the future of the Methodist Church itself.

For Gatehead the year 2012 is decisive. Both numbers and financial resources have been severely depleted and each church council meeting must now ask itself 'can we go on for another six months?' The last members of the chapel, many related by blood or marriage to the first, have fought valiantly to maintain its witness in the locality. It is still viewed as their family church by large numbers of people, who return for funerals, christenings and other occasional services and it is undoubtedly held in high esteem and affection by them. But will the 'light on a hill' still be seen for miles around when Gatehead celebrates its two-hundredth anniversary in just twenty-four years time?

Figure 43. The Lenten Cross

96

Ministers at Gatehead

dating from the creation of the Scholes Primitive Methodist Circuit

1878	Mr Gregory	1948	W Pollard
1886	Isaiah Potts	1952	J A Sollitt
1890	T Rushworth	1953	K A Wade
1893	Francis Leadby	1957	G N Beardslcy
1896	J Binns	1960	P E Gooch
1899	R E Wheeler	1961	D Taylor-Clarke
1902	C Ball	1964	F Turner
1903	W Kitchen	1968	W Burton
1906	H Preston	1969	S Hatcher
1908	W R Brotherton	1972	Haigh Jowett
1911	J H Robertshaw	1973	S Brown
1918	T H Brady	1974	J Furbank
1919	A Naylor	1976	Philip Auden
1922	P Shaw	1978	C Wilson
1926	B W Tinkler	1984	B Newbold
1933	P E Cooper	1985	Eric Foreman
1934	W T Rose	1988	James Skinner
1935	G H Rigale	1993	Judith Chapman
1936	W W Perris	1998	William Porter
1941	P D Robert	2003	Diane Hicks
1945	J W Almond	2008	Tim Moore

Illustrations

Map of Gatehead and district by the author.

Figures 1, 2, 5, 12, 16 and 22 with kind permission of Mr Leslie Robinson, proprietor of the Textile Heritage Centre in Skelmanthorpe.

Figures 6, 9, 14, 15, 17, 20, 23, 24, 37 and 40 with kind permission of Mr Leslie Tinker.

Figures 7, 11, 13, 18, 21, 25, 26, 29, 30, 31, 32, 33, 34, 35, 36, 38, 39, 42 and 43 with kind permission of Mr Jeffrey Turner.

Figure 10 published in *Chapels and Churches of the New Mill Valley* by Pamela Cooksey and used with her permission.

Figure 41 with kind permission of Mrs Lorna Stanley.

Figures 3, 8, 19, 27 and 28 from author's own collection.

Figure 4 image in the public domain.

Front cover illustration from a painting by Harold Battye, showing the old chapel and the then Sunday school at Gatehead, (with the kind permission of Mr Jeffrey Turner).

Back cover photograph with kind permission of Mr Jeffrey Turner.

(Endnotes)

i   Kendall, Holliday Bickerstaff, *The Origin and History of the Primitive Methodist Church*, London, 1919, p.3.

ii   Sykes, D F E, LL.B, *Huddersfield and its Vicinity*, Huddersfield, 1898, p.251.

iii   *Ibid.*, p.256.

iv   *Ibid.*, p.264.

v   *Ibid.*, p.257.

vi   Williams, Eileen, *Holmfirth, from forest to township*, Huddersfield, 1975, p.115.

vii   Sykes, *op cit*, p.267.

viii   *Ibid.*, p.313ff.

ix   *Ibid.*, p.317ff.

x   Kendall, *op cit*, p.1.

xi   Ritson, Joseph, *The Romance of Primitive Methodism*, London, 1910, p.7.

xii   Cook, Paul E G, *Fire from Heaven; times of extraordinary revival,* Darlington, 2009, p.20.

xiii   Kendall, *op cit*, p.2ff.

xiv   Ashworth, Jesse, *The Life of the Venerable Hugh Bourne*, London, 1888, p.23.

xv   Kendall, *op cit*, p.13.

xvi   *Ibid.*, p.24.

xvii   *Ibid.*, p.18.

xviii   Ritson, *op cit*, p.162.

xix   *The Primitive Methodist magazine*, 1843, p.123.

xx   Family history of the Hinchliffes of Denby Dale in author's private collection.

xxi   *Ibid.*

xxii   *The Primitive Methodist magazine*, 1843, p.124.

xxiii   *Ibid.*

xxiv   Heath, Chris, *Denby and District II: from landed lords to inspired industrialists*, Wharncliffe Books, 2004, p.95.

xxv   *Ibid.*

xxvi   Williams, *op cit*, p.127.

xxvi   Kendall, *op cit*, p.64.

xxviii   Letter from Jeremiah Gilbert to his mother, dated 24th May 1821, published in the Barnsley Times, 28th Jan 1876.

xxix   http://www.bradwellinpeak.f9.co.uk/firstprim.htm

xxx   *The Primitive Methodist magazine*, 1838, p.103.

xxxi Kirklees Community History Service, *Methodist Churches In Kirklees*, 2000.

xxxii *Ibid*, p.104.

xxxiii *Ibid*, p.104.

xxxiv Morehouse, Henry James, *History of Kirkburton and the Graveship of Holme*, Huddersfield, 1861, p.201.

xxxv Raymonds Original Pollbooks, *The Yorkshire West Riding Poll Book 1835*, Exeter.

xxxvi Morehouse, *op cit*, p.200.

xxxvii *Graveship of Holme Inclosure Award 1834*, West Yorkshire Archives, Kirklees.

xxxviii Hunt, Robert, *Geological Survey of Great Britain*, HMSO, 1866, p.155.

xxxix Ritson, *op cit*, p.226ff.

xl Battye, Harold, *Gatehead Methodist Church - 150ᵗʰ Anniversary Souvenir, 1836 – 1986*, Holmfirth, 1986, p.11.

xli *The Primitive Methodist magazine*, 1878, p.437.

xlii Battye, Harold, *Gatehead Methodist Church: Centenary Souvenir*, Holmfirth, 1936, p.6.

xliii *Ibid*, p.7.

xliv Cooksey, Pamela, *Chapels and Churches of the New Mill Valley*, Honley, 2009, p.37.

xlv Cook, *op cit*, pp.105-6.

xlvi Mallinson, Joel, *Methodism in Huddersfield, Holmfirth and Denby Dale*, London, 1898, p.51.

xlvii Battye, *150ᵗʰ Anniversary Souvenir, op cit*, p.12.

xlviii Battye, *Centenary Souvenir, op cit, p.8*.

xlix Letter from Mr James N Kaye, dated 1985, in the private collection of Mr Jeffrey Turner.

l Battye, *150ᵗʰ Anniversary Souvenir, op cit*, p.16.

li *Ibid*, p.26.

lii Mallinson, *op cit*, p.40.

liii Hunt, *op cit*, p.155.

liv Winstanley, Ian, ed., *Children's Employment Commission 1842*, Picks Publishing, 1997, www.cmhrc.co.uk

lv *Ibid.*, p.142.

lvi *Ibid.*, p.16.

lvii *Ibid.*, p.61.

lviii *Ibid.*, p.28.

lix Battye, *150ᵗʰ Anniversary Souvenir, op cit*, p.5.

lx	Higginson, Frank, *Upperthong Sunday School, centenary souvenir handbook*, Holmfirth, 1937, p.18.
lxi	Winstanley, *op cit*, p.143.
lxii	http://www.vintageinn.co.uk/thesovereignshepley/
lxiii	Letter from Mr James N Kaye, dated 1985, in the private collection of Mr Jeffrey Turner.
lxiv	Winstanley, *op cit*, p.26.
lxv	Sykes, *op cit*, p.359.
lxvi	*The Huddersfield Daily Chronicle*, Monday, March 21st, 1887; page 4; issue 6124.
lxvii	*The Huddersfield Daily Chronicle*, Monday, October 13th, 1890; page 3; issue 7238.
lxviii	*The Huddersfield Daily Chronicle*, Tuesday, May 19th, 1885; page 3; issue 5551.
lxix	*The Lindleys of Hepworth*, MS, HDFHS, Meltham.
lxx	*The Primitive Methodist magazine*, 1874, p.567.
lxxi	*The Lindleys of Hepworth*, MS, HDFHS, Meltham.
lxxii	Ritson, Joseph, *op cit*, p.283.
lxxiii	Letter from Mr J N Kaye, dated August 1985, in the private collection of Mr Jeffrey Turner.
lxxiv	*Ibid.*
lxxv	www.spartacus.schoolnet.co.uk/EDsunday.htm
lxxvi	Battye, *Centenary Souvenir*, *op cit*, p.11.
lxxvii	Winstanley, *op cit*, p.30.
lxxviii	*Ibid.*, p.31.
lxxix	*Ibid.*, p.143ff.
lxxx	*Ibid.*, p.33.
lxxxi	Hughes, Rev. Joseph, *The history of the township of Meltham, near Huddersfield*, Huddersfield, 1866, p.189.
lxxxii	Battye, Harold, *150th Anniversary Souvenir*, *op cit*, p.7.
lxxxiii	Battye, Harold, *Gatehead Methodist Sunday School Jubilee Souvenir*, Holmfirth, 1982.
lxxxiv	*Huddersfield Chronicle*, 31st May 1856, 19th Century British Library Newspapers.
lxxxv	*Ibid.*
lxxxvi	Battye, Harold, *Gatehead Methodist Sunday School Jubilee Souvenir, op cit.*
lxxxvii	Letter from Mr James N Kaye, dated 1985, in the private collection of Mr Jeffrey Turner.
lxxxviii	Battye, Harold, *Gatehead Methodist Sunday School Jubilee Souvenir, op cit.*

lxxxix	http://www.quickregister.net/links/article.php?id=21
xc	Kendall, *op cit*, p.156.
xci	1907 Primitive Methodist Conference resolution
xcii	*Ibid.*
xciii	*Ibid.*
xciv	http://en.wikipedia.org/wiki/Battle_of_Arras_(1917)#Second_Battle_of_Bullecourt_.=283.E2.80.9317_May_19 17.29
xcv	Kendall, *op cit*, p.169.
xcvi	*Ibid.*, p.170. Lines from *Safety* by Rupert Brooke, 1914.
xcvii	Wheeler, Hazel, *Huddersfield at War*, Stroud, 1992, p.5.
xcviii	*Holmfirth Express*, 2nd September 1939.
xcix	http://www.bbc.co.uk/bradford/peoples_war/ww2.shtml
c	*Holmfirth Express*, 23rd March 1940.
ci	'A British party game in which one draws a beetle in parts'. (Wikipedia)
cii	Heath, *op cit*, p.100.
ciii	*Ibid.*, p.100 ff.
civ	Battye, Harold, *Gatehead Methodist Church - 150th Anniversary Souvenir, op cit*, p.21.
cv	*Huddersfield Examiner*, March 1932; newspaper cutting in the private collection of Mr Jeffrey Turner.
cvi	http://christianbookshelf.org/schaff/the_creeds_of_the_evangelical_protestant_churches/methodist_church_union_in_england.htm
cvii	*The Lindleys of Hepworth*, MS, HDFHS, Meltham.
cviii	http://en.wikipedia.org/wiki/Winter_of_1946%E2%80%931947_in_the_United_Kingdom
cix	http://www.openwriting.com/archives/2004/02/sledging_to_sch.php
cx	Battye, Harold, *Gatehead Methodist Church - 150th Anniversary Souvenir, op cit*, p.23.
cxi	Press cutting in the private collection of Mr Jeffrey Turner.
cxii	*Holmfirth Express*, 25th April 1986.
cxiii	*Ibid.*
cxiv	Battye, Harold, *Gatehead Methodist Church - 150th Anniversary Souvenir, op cit*, p.26.
cxv	Price, Dave, *Turning the world upside down*, p.100, http://daves-little-blog.blogspot.co.uk/p/book-preview-turning-world-upside-down.htm